Egyptian Hieroglyphs for Complete Beginners

BILL MANLEY

EGYPTIAN HIEROGLYPHS FOR COMPLETE BEGINNERS

47 illustrations

T&H

Magic words for Harry

Title page Hieroglyphs on the stela of Shenwy, UC14334, in the Petrie Museum of Egyptian Archaeology, University College London (detail from image on page 68).

First published in the United Kingdom in 2012 by Thames & Hudson Ltd, 181A High Holborn, London WC1V 7QX

First published in the United States of America in 2012 by Thames & Hudson Inc., 500 Fifth Avenue, New York, New York 10110

Reprinted with corrections 2013
Reprinted 2022

British Library Cataloguing-in-Publication Data
A catalogue record for this book is available from the British Library

Library of Congress Control Number 2011936390

ISBN 978-0-500-05172-6 (UK hardcover)
ISBN 978-0-500-29028-6 (US paperback)

Printed and bound in China by Everbest Printing Co. Ltd

FSC www.fsc.org MIX From responsible sources FSC® C124385

CONTENTS

Preface

This book is a doorway to the ancient past. Its only intention is to give you the confidence to begin reading the hieroglyphic monuments of Ancient Egypt. Such an attractive and compelling script is more straightforward to read than you may suppose – with the help of an effective guide. So the following pages explain and illustrate the basic reading skills clearly, and let you move forward at your own pace. Your first steps are bound to be a little disorientated and wobbly, but practice makes perfect. Work spaces have been provided so you can practise what you have learned and measure your progress. Once you have managed to read as far as the stela of Minuser on page 44, you may start to stride forward. Once you have read to the end, then the statues of pharaohs and the tombs and coffins of their officials will have begun to make sense to you. If the ancient world interests you, what pleasure will you find in reading these inscriptions for yourself?

The way this book works assumes you have no particular knowledge of any foreign language, ancient or modern, and no particular knowledge of grammar or specialized terminology. It is founded on the author's 25 years' experience of teaching hieroglyphs to students with no previous knowledge of the subject. At amateur societies, summer schools and universities, hundreds of folk have learned how to read ancient inscriptions using the approach set out here. Convenient pathways for progress have become apparent and added to the course of study, while common obstacles have been identified and taken into account. A lot has been gained from the feedback of adult learners.

Rather than being laid out as a traditional grammar book or a primer, the approach here has been organized around a sequence of monuments, which you are invited to examine and read right from the start. The things you need to know in order to do so have been explained in a clear and

accessible manner. The inscriptions have been broken down into individual words using a graphic presentation. From the very first monument – a stela of a man called Mereri, who died 4,000 years ago – the emphasis is entirely on reading ancient inscriptions, not learning jargon. There are no tests or exercises as such, but there is plenty of practice in reading the real thing and you are able to check your own readings against the full explanations and translations given here. Remember, this is a guide rather than a grammar, but you may trust that it is a reliable guide.

The monuments have been selected across two millennia, from about 3000 to about 1100 BC. Hopefully such a vast time span will allow you to feel a sense of engagement with the sheer antiquity of Egypt. (In the 1st millennium BC the way words were written in hieroglyphs began to change in subtle ways, so we will not worry about monuments from that era here.) You are invited to read inscriptions of high officials, as well as monuments of kings, including some from the earliest times and some of the most celebrated. By the end of the book, you will have the knowledge and skills to make sense of the inscriptions most commonly found in tombs, on the statues and obelisks of kings, and the accounts of life and death most often displayed in museums with Ancient Egyptian collections.

Through these inscriptions you can also explore the interplay between art and hieroglyphs, and what this tells us about ancient beliefs in gods, kings and life after death. The elegance of hieroglyphic monuments is such that this book could hardly fail to be attractively illustrated and here you will find a wealth of clear photographs and newly commissioned drawings. For most of the latter, the author is indebted to Claire Gilmour of East Ayrshire Museums.

No writing system is entirely logical and hieroglyphic writing may often defy your expectations. Never fear. The

appropriate response is to keep your expectations to the minimum, study the inscriptions carefully, and allow yourself to be guided with an open mind. You will find here a clear explanation of some 25 ancient monuments, each of which in turn serves as a good example of the type of monument you are most likely to encounter in a museum or on a trip to Egypt. You can be confident of learning fundamental skills that enable you to read the inscriptions and encourage you to go further.

More information about museums with Ancient Egypt collections is available from CIPEG (http://cipeg.icom.museum) and the Fitzwilliam Museum, Cambridge (www.fitzmuseum.cam.ac.uk/er/museum.html). Local societies devoted to Ancient Egypt may be found via sites such as Egyptologists Electronic Forum (www.egyptologyforum.org), Osiris Net (www.osirisnet.net), and Ancient Egypt Magazine (www.ancientegyptmagazine.com). There are other Egyptian language resources and forums on the internet, but standard caveats apply regarding the variable quality of what is available. Last but not least are the monuments and museums of Egypt, which you can learn about directly from the Ministry of State for Antiquities (www.sca-egypt.org).

Reading ancient inscriptions is a valuable skill, and this book provides first steps, not an account of the full complexity of Ancient Egyptian. Some 'rules' you are given at the beginning of the book get qualified later, when you are better able to comprehend what is going on. None the less, in just a hundred and fifty pages, you are set to begin a journey of many centuries.

INSCRIPTIONS

Stela of Mereri from his Tomb at Dendereh (6th Dynasty, *c.* 2200 BC)

1 Stela of Mereri, from Dendereh
❶ An offering which the king gives Osiris / ❷ lord of Djedu: a voice offering for / ❸ the governor, overseer of priests, guardian of the temple cattle / ❹ Mereri

#1 What You Need to Know: Sound Signs

Let us begin a journey into ancient times by making sense of this stela from the tomb of Mereri, one of a pair in this book (we will come to the other on page 34). An Ancient Egyptian stela is a stone block, usually from a tomb, inscribed with hieroglyphs and images, while this particular one is now in the National Museum of Scotland, Edinburgh.

The first thing you need to know is that hieroglyphs are not a kind of picture writing. Knowing what a particular hieroglyph *shows* gives you no clue about how to read it. For example, look carefully at the stela of Mereri. On the left you can see the slender, muscular figure of the man himself, in his fine kilt and collar and official's wig. He carries a staff and sceptre as symbols of his authority. In front of him, four columns of hieroglyphs promise to tell us something about the man and his monument; but what are the hieroglyphs? An eye and a hand, a brace of birds, a couple of seated men, half a lion and a cow – and so on. What sense would you make from these pictures? Certainly not the correct reading, which you can also see in the caption opposite.

So how do we come by the correct reading? The key is to understand that most hieroglyphs write sounds in the Egyptian language. For example, an owl does not mean 'owl': it writes the sound '*m*'. You do not need to know why it writes '*m*', any more than you need to know why (in the English alphabet) we use the shape M. It is what we are taught to do. Likewise, just learn that the owl hieroglyph writes the sound '*m*' (and the best way to learn it is to copy it out a few times). Here are 16 hieroglyphs that write sounds you know from English:

𓇌 or 𓏭	pair of leaves/strokes	*y*	𓂋	mouth	*r*
𓅱	quail chick	*w*	𓉔	fence (seen from above)	*h*
𓃀	lower leg	*b*	𓋴 or 𓊃	folded cloth/door bolt	*s*
𓊪	mat	*p*	𓎡	dish	*k*
𓆑	viper	*f*	𓎼	pot stand	*g*
𓅓	owl	*m*	𓏏	small loaf	*t*
𓈖	water ripple	*n*	𓂧	hand	*d*

In addition, these three hieroglyphs write sounds you know well, but we do not have special letters for them in the English alphabet:

𓈙	lake	*š*	'sh' in *ship*.
𓍿	animal tether	*ṯ*	soft 't' in *adventure*, similar to 'ch' in *church*.
𓆓	snake	*ḏ*	soft 'd', similar to 'j' of *jail*.

It is important to recognize that *s* and *š* are different sounds, just as *t* and *ṯ* are different and *d* and *ḏ* are different. We use the special marks (called diacritics) above and below the letters to indicate the differences.

Now, in just a few moments you have already learned 19 different hieroglyphs and the sounds that they write. Finally, here are seven hieroglyphs that write sounds we do not usually recognize in English:

𓄿	vulture	ꜣ	(Called *alif.*) The stop in the middle of *uh oh* or Cockney pronunciation of *bottle* as *bo-ul.*
𓇋	reed leaf	ỉ	(Called *yodh.*) The weak 'y' sound at the end of *tea* (think, half of 𓇌 y above). Not to be confused with English *i.*
𓂝	forearm	ꜥ	(Called *ayin.*) Throaty gurgle, like saying *a* while swallowing.
𓎛	wick of flax	ḥ	(Called 'second *h*'.) Breathy *h* pronounced in the throat.
𓐍	ball of twine	ḫ	(Called 'third *h*'.) Scots 'ch' in *loch.*
𓄡	animal belly	ẖ	(Called 'fourth *h*'.) Softer than *ḫ*, like German 'ch' in *ich.*
𓈎	hill slope	ḳ	(Called *qaf.*) Arabic 'q' in *Qurãn.* Like '*k*', but pronounced further back in the mouth.

The last seven sounds may seem offputting, but, remember, you do not have to learn how to *speak* Egyptian (Arabic became the principal language of Egypt about a thousand years ago, and Egyptian is no longer *spoken* or read by anyone there). All you need to do is recognize these sounds wherever they are written.

Some folk find a particular problem recognizing that *h, ḥ, ḫ* and *ẖ* are different sounds in Egyptian. Maybe this illustration will help:

ḥr = above

ḫr = before 

ẖr = beneath

You can see here three different words in Egyptian, with three different meanings and three different sounds. So you must be able to distinguish *ḥr* from *ḫr* or *ẖr*, when the time comes to read them in hieroglyphs (you will do this soon). Because *h, ḥ, ḫ* and *ẖ* are different sounds, there are different hieroglyphs to write them.

The sounds '*i*' and '*w*' are called 'weak' sounds. This is because they are often simply dropped from the writing, especially when they appear at the beginning or the end of a word. This is presumably because they were also often dropped in speaking.

Now practise what you have learned:

– 1-sound signs

....

....

....

....

....

....

....

....

....

DID YOU KNOW?

As you can see on the stela of Mereri, the hieroglyph of an owl is carefully drawn showing the bird's feathers. The artists frequently drew or cut hieroglyphs with great care and attention, showing the features of an animal or object in such detail that we can often identify the species of an animal. As a result, we get an insight into the ancient conception of writing as an aspect of art.

#2 What You Need to Know: Direction of Writing

Now you know the 24 sounds normally written in the Egyptian language, and 26 hieroglyphs that can write them (remember and both write *y*, while and both write *s*). These are 1-sound hieroglyphs, because they each write one sound. Look back at Mereri's stela and see how many of these hieroglyphs you can find. You will not be able to read any words yet, but you can find nine of these hieroglyphs, including a couple used more than once. What the other hieroglyphs are doing, we will come back to soon.

Something else you will notice: the hieroglyphs face the opposite way to those we have learned. We know that writes *m*, but in column 3 of the stela we find instead. What difference does this make? The answer is, none at all. Egyptian hieroglyphs can be written from the left (as we write) or from the right (as in Mereri's stela) without this affecting their meaning. How do we know which way to read? Any hieroglyph with a front or a face will look towards the beginning of the text. (In fact, if you were asked to draw a face you would probably draw it something like this , facing left because you are used to writing from the left.) In the stela, you can see that the birds and animals – and, indeed, the figure of Mereri himself – all *look to the right*, so we start reading *at the right*. On the other hand, when we are explaining things in this book we will normally write the hieroglyphs from the left because then they follow the direction of the English text.

Back to the stela: the words have been divided into four columns using vertical lines. Again, hieroglyphic texts can be written horizontally (along a line) or vertically (in a column), and it is usually obvious which way to read. The only thing you need to remember here is that hieroglyphs written in columns always read *from top to bottom* (never upwards), so when you see a hieroglyph above another one, read the top one first. For example, let us go back to the illustration above and add some hieroglyphs:

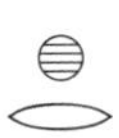
ẖr = before

Here the word *ẖr* 'before' is written with one hieroglyph above another, and we read the top hieroglyph first.

To illustrate how this works, let us look at a stela of the 1st millennium BC in the Metropolitan Museum of Art, New York. It is beautifully painted, with boxes marked out for hieroglyphic texts. However, the hieroglyphs were never actually painted in, perhaps because the intended recipient died before the work could be finished.

DID YOU KNOW?

Although we cannot be sure why, this stela is obviously not finished. Many monuments have come down to us incomplete, not least because archaeologists occasionally find artists' workshops. More often, inscriptions on stelae and tomb walls, including tombs in the Valley of the Kings near Thebes, have been found where, in some sections, the hieroglyphs have only been sketched out or where craftsmen have just done the initial rough work.

2 Unfinished stela in the Metropolitan Museum of Art.

You can see from the blank boxes how the hieroglyphic texts would have been laid out. One box sits above the head of the man holding a pair of incense burners and doubtless this text would have told us who he was. Probably the hieroglyphs in the box would have read from left to right (as indicated by the arrow), so that they face the same way as the man. The other block of hieroglyphs would have told us about the strange-looking god seated on the throne. (He is actually the funerary god, Sokar, who has a mummified body and the head of a falcon.) Notice how the block has been arranged to read in front of his face, then 'wrap' down in front of the enthroned god. This creates a right-angled block ⁊↓ because that shape fills the available space, and other stelae show us that the block would have been filled with writing in lines and columns (as shown by the arrows), or perhaps just with two or three columns of writing.

Internet Café

This last point explains why hieroglyphs can be written horizontally and vertically: sculptors liked to fill the available space as fully and effectively as required. They arranged texts in ways that suited the monuments they decorated. Hieroglyphs are beautiful to look at because they are meant to dignify the sacred sites of the Ancient Egyptians – their temples and tombs. To do so included organizing hieroglyphs into pleasing and attractive arrangements, which followed the lines of the artwork. In Mereri's stela, you can see how the columns follow the upright figure, and how the columns read naturally from the right so that they finish at the image of Mereri himself. The notion of writing in different directions may seem odd at first, but think how easily you can read a sign like the one on the left. You will soon get used to reading hieroglyphs in different directions without giving the matter a second thought.

Now, here are two words that appear on Mereri's stela:

 n for  temple cattle

Study them, then find where they are written on the stela (at the ends of columns 2 and 3). Remember, the hieroglyphs are arranged vertically in the stela. Ignore any hieroglyphs that did not appear among the 26 above ( and) because these will be explained on page 18.

#3 Vowels and Pronunciation

You have just met the word 'for' in Egyptian, which is written with the sound '*n*', while the word for 'temple cattle' is written with the sounds *ṯntt*. They have both been written without vowels; that means without the sounds we write in English using the letters A, E, I, O and U. Vowels are sounds we make by keeping our mouths and throats open when speaking and they are crucial for pronouncing words. Therefore, Egyptian when spoken had vowels, but they are rarely written down in hieroglyphs. So rarely, in fact, that we do not have to worry about them in this book. As a result, words written in hieroglyphs may seem like word skeletons (or text messages), as though we were to write *ppl cn rd ths* ('people can read this'). Likewise, the stela gives us only the skeleton of *ṯntt* and we do not know how it was pronounced. This is a frustrating aspect of hieroglyphic texts, but one we cannot wish away.

You do not need to speak Egyptian, so pronunciation is not relevant to making sense of what you are reading. In classrooms or study groups, many folk like to insert a brief 'e' where necessary into words so they can be spoken aloud, in which case *ṯntt* is pronounced something like 'chentet'. Likewise, ꜣ and ꜥ may be pronounced as 'a' because they are foreign sounds for us, while *ỉ* may be pronounced as 'i', and *w* may be pronounced as 'u'. In this way, *ỉnpw* may be spoken aloud as 'inpu'. However, this is purely a convenience for use among ourselves and does not bear much relation to how words were actually spoken in ancient times.

Here are more words written in hieroglyphs, which appear in inscriptions you are going to read later in the book. Work out which sounds appear in each word, and compare your own readings with the answers (or cover up the answers, if you prefer). Remember, ignore for now any hieroglyphs that did not appear above – they will be explained below (see **#4**):

	*ỉnpw*	Anubis (god)	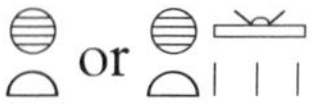	*ḫt*	thing
	*ywỉꜣ*	Yuia (name)	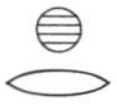	*ḫr*	before
	*pt*	sky	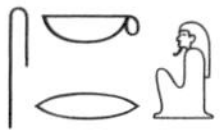	*skr*	Sokar (god)
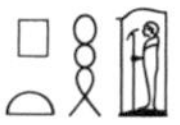	*ptḥ*	Ptah (god)		*sgrḥ*	pacify
	*f*	he/his	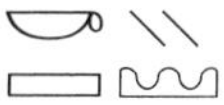	*kšy*	Kush (place)
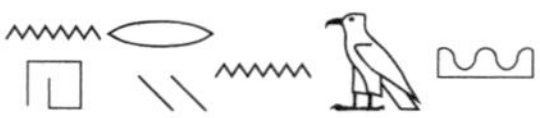	*nhrynꜣ*	Naharin (place)		*ty*	Ty (name)
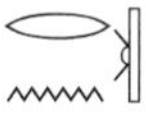	*rn*	name		*ṯwỉꜣ*	Tjuia (name)

#4 What You Need to Know: Determinatives

The hieroglyphs you have learned so far write sounds in the Egyptian language, and you have seen how they can be put together to write words such as *ṯntt*. We have also seen *ṯntt* written as  on Mereri's stela. If the first four hieroglyphs write the sounds *ṯntt*, what are the last two hieroglyphs doing? Well, this is the second use of hieroglyphs: instead of writing sounds, some hieroglyphs tell us about the meaning of the word. The sign tells us this is a word for 'cattle' and the sign (which can also appear as ꜣ ꜣ ꜣ) tells us that this is a word for a group or herd (three strokes indicate the plural or anything that involves 'more than just one and more than a pair', see also **#24**). Hieroglyphs used in this way are called *determinatives* because they help us 'determine' what the word means.

Determinatives are generally written at the end of words, so they help us break a text up into individual words, which is useful because there are no commas or spaces between words in Egyptian inscriptions. Here are the other determinatives in Mereri's stela:

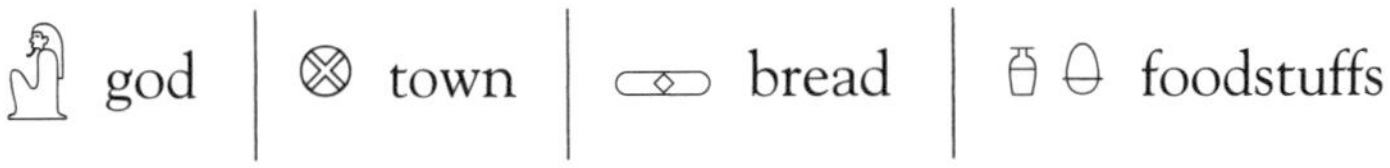

Determinatives are not usually specific to one word, so may appear in any word to do with a god or the name of any god, while may appear in the name of any town. A word may have two or three determinatives. On the other hand, no word *has* to be written with a determinative. For example, you have already seen the word *n* 'for' written with a sound sign and nothing else. Nevertheless, when determinatives are written they are very helpful.

DID YOU KNOW ?

The thoughtful interplay between sacred art and hieroglyphs is quite obvious on the stela of Mereri. Notice how the four columns of the inscription are organized by using vertical lines, the last of which is formed by the staff in Mereri's hand. This staff then isolates a small group of hieroglyphs next to Mereri himself, and these are the very ones that write his name. It is not easy to say where the picture ends and the writing begins. In fact, the word 'hieroglyph', taken from Greek, means 'sacred image' (not writing), while hieroglyphic inscriptions in Ancient Egypt were sometimes described as 'divine words'.

So now look for where determinatives appear in Mereri's stela because you know they probably mark the ends of various words.

Here are some other common determinatives, which also appear in this book:

	name / occupation of men		name / occupation of women
	dignitary / the dead		raised / high
	strike / force		strike / force
	gesture / calm	or	bread / foodstuff
	sky / above		land, especially desert
or	minerals / pigments		land / earth
	tree		water
	building		granite
	cup / fluid		foreign (the throw-stick is a non-Egyptian weapon)

Pay special attention to the following three determinatives:

used in the word or *ỉt* 'father' and nowhere else, this sign looks the same as the 1-sound sign *f*, but presumably was originally a different sign (see page 126)

or (papyrus scroll) used to write words for ideas we cannot picture but we can write down, such as *ḫt* 'thing' or *rn* 'name'

or used with a group / herd / plural (see **#24**)

You may be surprised to learn that you are already only two steps away from knowing all about how hieroglyphs are used to write the text on Mereri's stela. At this point, you may like to go back to the stela and make sure you are clear about what you recognize. In **#6**, we will move onto the hieroglyphs you do not recognize yet: what are they doing? In the meantime, here is a question for you to think about.

#5 How Do We Know How to Read Hieroglyphs?

You may well wonder, how do we know that hieroglyphs usually write sounds in Egyptian? The first indication is the one we noted above: if we treat hieroglyphs as picture writing (remember the owl sign writing '*m*' on page 13 above), it is very difficult to make sense of what any text means. This is even more the case when we compare one text with another, where some of the same hieroglyphs appear, but in different combinations and consistent translations become impossible. For many centuries after the ancient knowledge of how to read Egyptian hieroglyphs was lost, hieroglyphs were treated by Egyptian and European scholars alike as picture writing, and the result was a proliferation of unlikely and contradictory theories.

However, during the first half of the 19th century a consensus emerged among those studying hieroglyphic inscriptions that they wrote a language; and, more to the point, a language very close to one already known well. The well-known language is Coptic, which was the indigenous language of Egypt during Byzantine and Arab rule, until it was displaced by Arabic during the period AD 900 to 1200. Crucially, Coptic was written using a version of the Greek alphabet, so knowledge of how to read Coptic was never lost. Now, the word 'for' in Coptic is Ⲛ or ⲚⲀ (na), which compares to 𓈖 *n* above. Likewise, the word for 'he' is Ϥ (f), which is the same as 𓆑 *f* above. In fact, there are innumerable examples of words in Coptic that we also find written in hieroglyphs. Once we recognize that Egyptian and Coptic are closely related, we arrive at a way of reading hieroglyphs that applies consistently from text to text. As a result, during the past two centuries we have learned a tremendous amount in detail about how to read hieroglyphic inscriptions going back 5,000 years to the very dawn of history.

Of course, there are differences between Egyptian and Coptic, but we should think of the relationship between them in terms of the relationship between Latin and Italian: two languages spoken in the same country, where the later language obviously developed out of the earlier one. Moreover, this is a continuous written history, so there are hieroglyphic texts from Egypt as late as the 4th century AD, the era when Coptic texts begin to appear in significant numbers. Here are some other comparisons between Egyptian and Coptic using words you will come across elsewhere in this book, remembering that words in Egyptian were not written down with vowels (a, e, i, o, u):

Egyptian	Coptic			Egyptian	Coptic		
ỉt	ⲉⲓⲱⲧ	(yõt)	father	*ḥmt*	ϩⲓⲙⲉ	(hime)	wife
pt	ⲡⲉ	(pe)	sky	*ḥnḳt*	ϩⲛⲕⲉ	(hnke)	beer
ms	ⲙⲓⲥⲉ	(mise)	give birth	*ḫꜣ*	ϣⲟ	(sho)	thousand
nfr	ⲛⲟⲩϥⲉ	(noufe)	perfect	*ẖr*	ϧⲁⲣⲟ	(kharo)	under

#6 What You Need to Know: Signs Writing 2 or 3 Sounds

By now you have found signs that write the sounds on pages 11–12, and you have also found the determinatives on the stela. So why do you still not recognize most of the signs? Why can you not find any words other than *n* 'of' and *ṯntt* 'temple cattle'? Well, because most signs on Mereri's stela – indeed most hieroglyphs in general – do not write a single sound. Instead, they write *combinations of two or three sounds*. For example, look at the start of column 2, where you will find the word 𓎟 *nb* 'lord'. All that has happened here is that *the hieroglyph* 𓎟 *spells the two sounds n + b together* and in that order (it never spells *b* + *n*). How do you know that *nb* means 'lord'? Well, you simply have to learn this word in Egyptian.

It may seem peculiar to use a sign for *nb* when there are perfectly good hieroglyphs for *n* and *b* already. Why did the ancients not use an alphabet, when they had the chance? There are various reasons for this, but three of the most important are as follows. First, if we only had the 26 hieroglyphs on pages 11–12, then hieroglyphic monuments would look increasingly dull and repetitive. Second, it would be difficult to divide the inscription into separate words because there are no spaces between words and no punctuation marks, such as commas and stops. Imaginetryingtoreadwritinglikethisalltheti meitcanbedonebutitisveryhardevenwhenyougetusedtoit. Of course, we could suggest using spaces between words, but the Ancient Egyptians liked hieroglyphs to fill the available space without leaving blank, uninscribed stone. Two-sound hieroglyphs, especially combinations of 2-sound hieroglyphs, are distinctive, so they help you to find where words appear. The hieroglyph 𓎟 adds visual interest to the inscription, and makes it easier for you to locate words based on the sounds *n* + *b* together (at least, once you have learned what 𓎟 is used for). Third, a hieroglyph writing two sounds is very economical: 𓎟 on its own can write the word *nb* 'lord'. To take another analogy from text writing, do you not find 'gr8' quicker to write and perhaps more distinctive than 'great'?

Here are the other hieroglyphs on the stela of Mereri that spell two sounds together:

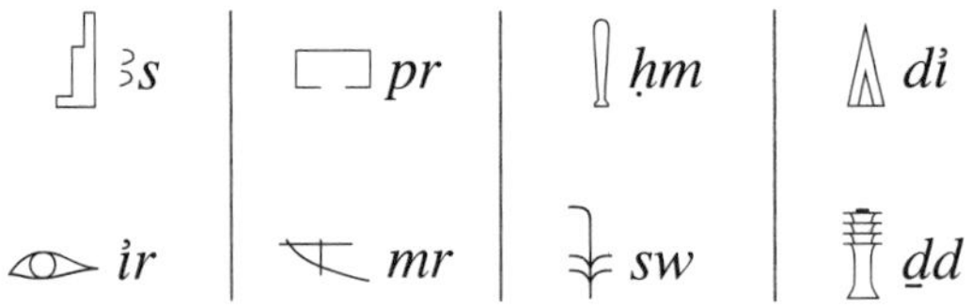

However, that is not the end of the matter. These hieroglyphs on his stela spell *three* sounds together:

No doubt, this last group of hieroglyphs seems like an unwelcome complication, but straight away there is good news. No hieroglyphs spell more than three sounds together. To put it another way, you now know all four different types of hieroglyphs that there are: those which write one sound, those which write two sounds, those which write three sounds, plus determinatives. Now you only have to practise and develop what you have learned so far. To that end, we now need to learn some more about how 2-sound and 3-sound hieroglyphs are used to write words.

DID YOU KNOW?

At least 700 different hieroglyphs were used to write Egyptian during the 2nd millennium BC and many new signs were devised throughout the centuries. Most people had no access to formal education, so literacy was a very limited skill identified more with power than education. In fact, the number of people who could read and write hieroglyphs was probably a fraction of 1%, most of them men. On the other hand, all of the kings of Egypt seem to have been literate unlike, for example, their contemporaries in Mesopotamia. As a result, all of the monuments you will read here belonged to high officials or the kings themselves. In general, these men, their families and priests were the intended audience.

#7 What You Need to Know: Sound Complements

What follows here is the most difficult idea you have to grasp when it comes to reading Egyptian. However, it is something that crops up a lot, so you are going to get a lot of practice. You will soon get the hang of it. In column 2, *nb* 'lord' appears as part of the common phrase *nb-ḏdw* (see below). Here you can also see the sound signs 𓊽 *ḏd* and 𓂧 *d* and 𓅱 *w*, plus the determinative 𓊖 for towns. So we seem to have a word with the sounds *ḏd* + *d* + *w*, while the determinative tells you that they spell the name of a town. However, here is a rule for you to learn:

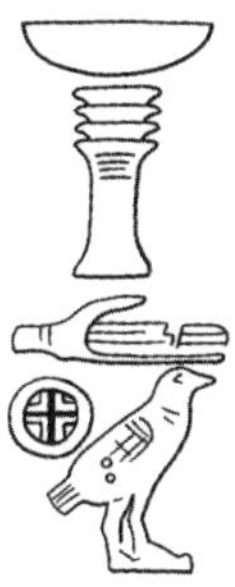

- When a 2-sound sign like 𓊽 is accompanied by a 1-sound sign like 𓂧 and the latter *matches* one of the sounds of the former, then the 1-sound sign *reinforces* the reading of the 2-sound sign. *It does not give new information, so we do not read it as a separate sound.* When hieroglyphs are used to reinforce the reading of another hieroglyph, we call them *sound complements*.

So what does this mean? In the inscription above we have 𓊽 *ḏd* followed by 𓂧 *d*. Does 𓂧 match any of the sounds of 𓊽? Yes, it does. So we read 𓊽𓂧 together as *ḏd*. Then we have 𓅱 *w*. Does this match any of the sounds of 𓊽? No, it does not. So 𓅱 gives us new information, and we can read *ḏdw*. This is the name of the town, which we know in English as Djedu. Therefore, the whole phrase written above is *nb-ḏdw*, which means 'lord of Djedu'. In Egyptian, titles often put words together without using 'of', just as we say goalkeeper ('keeper of the goal') or bank manager ('manager of a bank').

Over the page you will find some common 2-sound signs, which you need to get to know as you make your way through this book. Make a note of the page and keep coming back to it, until you have learned these hieroglyphs. You may also like to copy them out onto bits of paper, and put their readings on the back. Copying hieroglyphs is a good method of fixing them in your mind, and afterwards you can use the bits of paper as flashcards to practise your learning.

Common 2-sound Signs

	ꜣw		*mr*		*ḫꜥ*		*tꜣ*
	ꜣb or *mr*		*mr*		*ḫt*	or	*tꜣ*
	ꜣs		*mḥ*		*ẖr*		*tw*
	ib		*ms*		*sꜣ*		*ti*
	in		*nw*		*sw*		*tp*
	in		*nb*		*sp*		*tp*
	ir		*rs*		*sn*		*tm*
or	*ꜥꜣ*		*ḥm*		*sẖ*	or	*di*
	wꜥ		*ḥm*		*sṯ or st*		*ḏꜣ*
	bḥ		*ḥr*		*šn*		*ḏw*
	pr		*ḥs*		*šs*		*ḏr*
	mꜣ		*ḥḏ*		*kꜣ*		*ḏd*
	mn		*ḫꜣ*		*gb*		

Opposite you will find a list of words written with these 2-sound signs. The words appear in inscriptions in this book. Work out which sounds appear in each word, and compare your own readings with the answers.

There are a few words in the list that you need to study closely, while you are getting used to reading words written with sound complements:

- Both *sꜣ* 'son' and *gb* 'Geb' are written with birds, and perhaps your knowledge of ornithology is not sufficient to tell them apart (as it happens, the former is a duck, the latter a goose). However, in the case of at least, the appearance of tells you that the bird is more likely to be *gb* (which reads with *b*) than *sꜣ* (which does not have *b*).

- In *ꜣbḏw* 'Abydos', the sign can read *ꜣb* or *mr*, but the appearance of indicates that you should read the group as *ꜣb*.

List of Words Written with 2-sound Signs

	*ꜣbḏw*	Abydos (place)
	*ḫꜣ*	thousand
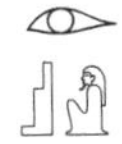	*ꜣsỉr*	Osiris (god)
	*ẖr*	beneath
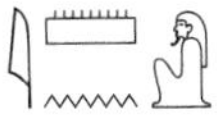	*ỉmn*	Amun (god)
	*sꜣ*	son
	*ỉntf*	Intef (name)
	*smr*	courtier
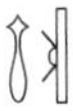 or 	*ꜥꜣ*	great
	*sn*	brother
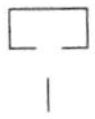	*pr*	estate
	*snỉ*	Seni (name)
	*mnṯw*	Montju (god)
	*sḥḏ*	controller
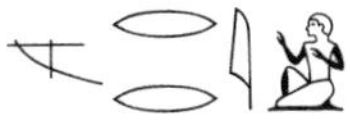	*mrrỉ*	Mereri (name)
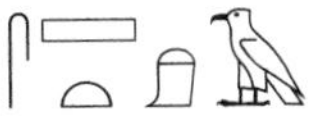	*sštꜣ*	secrets
	*ms*	born
	*šs*	alabaster
	*nb*	lord
	*kꜣ*	soul
	*nbtw*	Nebtu (name)
	*gb*	Geb (god)
	*ḥr*	above
	*tp*	upon
	*ḥry*	keeper (title)
 or 	*dỉ*	give
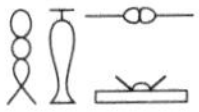	*ḥs*	praised
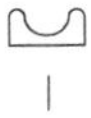	*dw*	hill
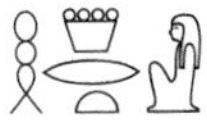	*ḥḏrt*	Hedjret (name)
	*ḏdw*	Djedu (place)

On the other hand, in the word *smr* 'courtier' you know the same sign is to be read *mr* because of the sound complement *r*. You see, sound complements actually help you to read words, once you get used to the way in which they are used.

- Read the name carefully. The sign gives you *mr*. Then you have *r*. Is this new information? No, and together read *mr*. However, you then find a second *r*. Is this new information? Yes, does not tell you that the name has two *r*'s, so a second does tell you something new. Finally, there is , and the whole name reads *mrrỉ* in Egyptian.

Two words written with a 2-sound sign are *ḥr* 'above/on' and *ẖr* 'beneath', so now we can complete the illustration from page 12:

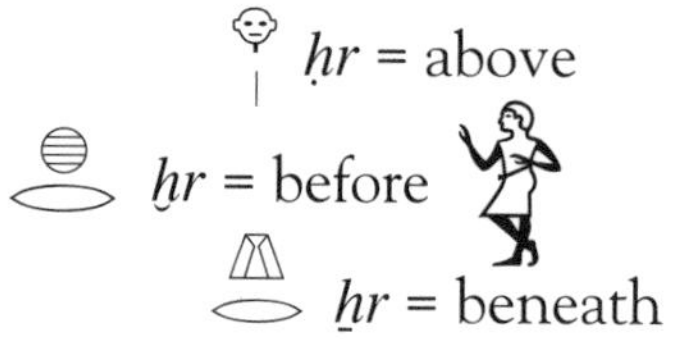

We can end this section by looking at most of the 3-sound signs used in this book and words written with them. Signs that write three sounds are helpful because they tend to write just one word or a single group of related words. For example, the sign writes the sounds *nfr*. These are found in *nfr* 'perfect', *nfrw* 'perfection' and other related words. However, few other words in Egyptian have the same three sounds in the same order. (How many English words can you think of with the three consonants *n* + *f* + *r* together and in that order? *Nefarious*, perhaps, or versions of *infer* and *confer*. In truth, there are not many.) So, although there is no visual link between and 'perfect', you can usually assume that writes the word *nfr* 'perfect'. Likewise, tends to write the word *ꜥnḫ* 'life', while tends to write the word *nṯr* 'god', and so on. Again, keep coming back to this table until you know these signs, and you may like to copy out these hieroglyphs and write their readings on the back.

Opposite you will also find some words that crop up in the book, written with 3-sound signs. In the usual way, work out which sounds appear in each word, then compare your own readings with the answers given here.

Common 3-sound Signs

Sign		Sign		Sign		Sign	
	ỉwn		*mꜣʿ*		*ḥḳꜣ*		*sꜣw*
	ỉdn		*mꜣẖ*		*ḥtp*		*stp*
	ʿnḫ		*mnw*		*ḫpr*		*sṯt*
	wꜣs		*nbw*		*ḫpš*		*šmʿ*
	wꜣḏ		*nfr*	or	*ḫnt*		*šnʿ*
	wʿb		*nḫb*		*ḫrw*	or	*ḳbḥ*
	wḥm		*nṯr*		*ḫtm*		*dwꜣ*
	wsr		*ḥꜣt*		*ẖnm*		*ḏsr*

Take care not to confuse *ꜣw* with *mꜣẖ* (the latter is really only used to write the word *ỉmꜣḫw* 'revered one', see page 45).

List of Words Written with 3-sound Signs

Hieroglyphs			Hieroglyphs		
	ỉwnw	Heliopolis (place)		*mꜣʿt*	order (see page 57)
	ỉmꜣḫw	revered one		*mnw*	Min (god)
	ỉdn	Iden (name)		*nbw*	gold
	ʿnḫ	life, live		*nfr*	perfect
	wꜣs	authority		*nḫbt*	Nekhbet (god)
	wꜣḏyt	Wadjyt (god)		*nṯr*	god
	wʿb	pure		*ḥḳꜣ*	ruler
	wḥmw	messenger		*ḥtp*	offering
	wsr	powerful		*ḫpr*	form

continued on page 28

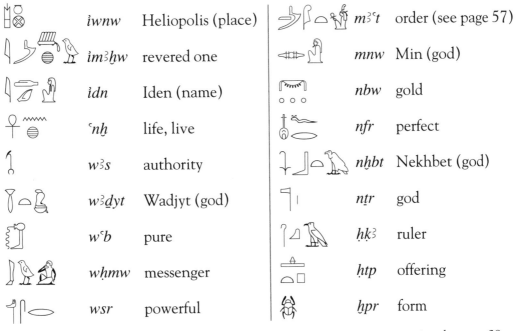

List of Words Written with 3-sound Signs *continued*

	*ḫpš*	strength
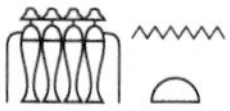	*ḫnt*	in front (of)
	*ḫrw*	voice
	*ḫnmw*	Khnum (god)
	*s3w*	guardian
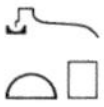	*stp*	choose
	*sṯtw*	Asiatics
	*šmꜥ*	south, Upper Egypt
	*šnꜥ*	storehouse
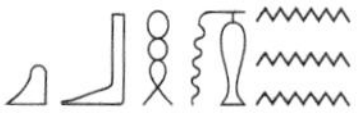	*ḳbḥw*	spring-water
	*dw3t*	adoration (see page 62)
	*ḏsr*	sacred

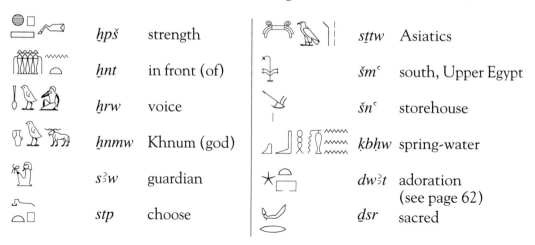

Notice that in the word *ḥtp* 'offering' there are sound complements with the sign *ḥtp*. Therefore, we can extend the rule on page 23:

- When a 3-sound sign like is accompanied by a 1-sound sign or a 2-sound sign and the latter *match* any of the sounds of the former, then the 1-sound sign or the 2-sound sign *reinforce* the reading of the 3-sound sign.

So what does this mean in practice? In the inscription above you have *ḥtp* followed by *t* and *p*. Does match any of the sounds of ? Yes, it does. Then you have *p*. Does this match any of the sounds of ? Yes, it does also. So you read together as *ḥtp*.

#8 What You Need to Know: Unexpected Writings

Now take a look at how Mereri's stela breaks down into words, so you can work out what the different hieroglyphs are doing. Remember, from page 10, the correct reading of the inscription is as follows:

❶ An offering which the king gives Osiris / ❷ lord of Djedu: a voice offering for / ❸ the governor, overseer of priests, guardian of the temple cattle / ❹ Mereri.

Hopefully you can see how most of these phrases have been written on the stela. For example, there are four columns of hieroglyphs, of which the fourth is a brief text isolated beside the figure of Mereri himself. This simply gives us

his name 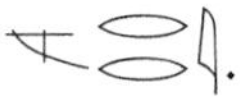. In column 3 we read that Mereri is *ḥ3ty-ʿ* 'governor'. He is also *m-r* 'overseer'. However, an overseer must oversee *somebody*, so, reading the next word, we also recognize that he is 'overseer of priests' (see right, remember titles in Egyptian do

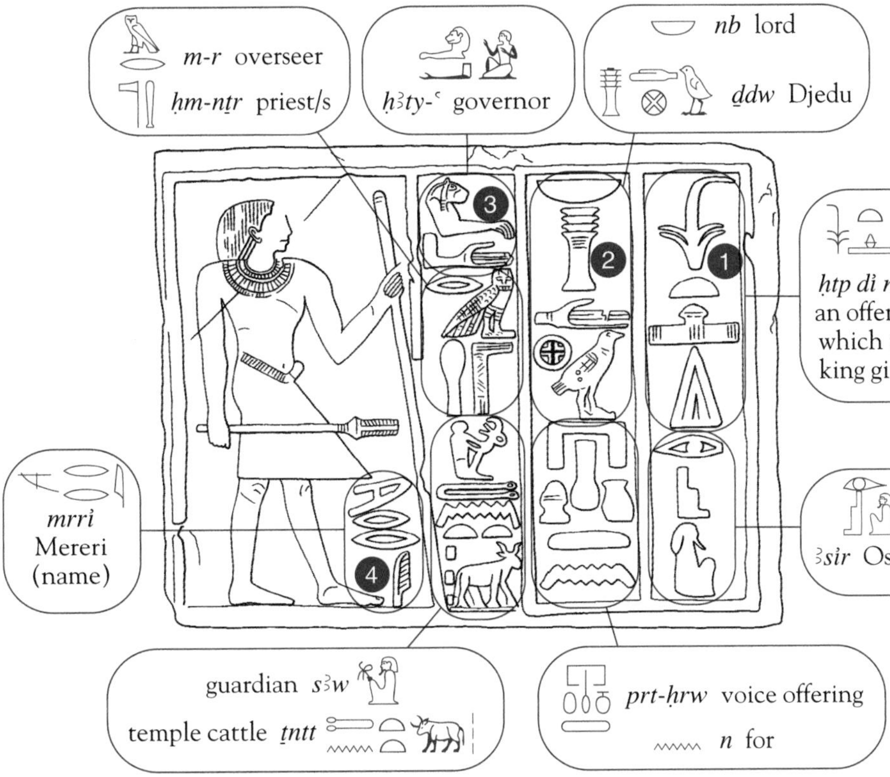

3 Stela of Mereri with the inscription explained.

not need to use a word for 'of'). He is also *s3w* 'guardian'. Again, a guardian must guard *something*, so we look at the next word and read *s3w ṯntt* 'guardian of temple cattle' (see left). Stop and think about this for a moment: even at this early stage, you can already read columns 3 and 4, and recognize most of the words in the first two columns.

On the other hand, there are words here that do not read as you may expect.

- In column 1, the name of the god of the dead, Osiris, is *3sir* in Egyptian. Therefore we may expect the writing to give us  *3s* followed by  *ir*, and, in fact, that is what usually happens. However, on the stela of

Mereri the signs are written the other way round (see right). None the less, it is the combination of the two signs that matters: both and are commonly used hieroglyphs, but the combination of and together tells us we have the name Osiris. Of course, the determinative clinches the matter.

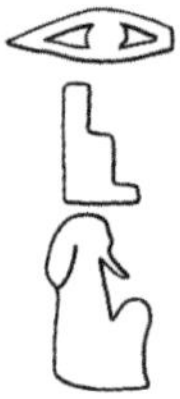

- The title 'overseer' seems to read *mr*, but you have been asked to read it as *m-r*. Why the hyphen? Well, this is because scholars have learned that this title is actually made up of two smaller words in Egyptian.

- Likewise, the title seems to write *ḥꜣtꜥ*, but you have been asked to read it as *ḥꜣty-ꜥ*. In this case the writing is an *abbreviation* of *ḥꜣty-ꜥ*. For the time being, you will have to take readings like this on trust, just as somebody learning English has to be taught that 'Dr' is an abbreviation of 'Doctor' and 'St' is another writing of 'Street'. We can be sure that is an abbreviation because occasionally on monuments the title is written out in full.

How could you know that is made up of two words? You could not – certainly not on the basis of what you have learned so far. Only many decades of scholarship have worked out the reading *m-r* (and, even then, some Egyptologists read the title slightly differently). Again, you will just have to take unexpected readings and abbreviations on trust. After all, how would you explain to somebody learning English that a 'TV' is the same thing as a 'telly'? The good news is that titles such as *m-r* are so common in inscriptions that you soon get to know them.

- In column 2 above we have a vertical writing of *ḏdw* (see right). The suggestion in **#4** was that determinatives will normally come at the end of words – and usually they do. However, as here, they do not have to. Why not? Well, if we look at *ḏdw* we have the signs *ḏd* and *w*, which are tall; between them we have *d*, which is flat; while the determinative is small. In the expected sequence the signs do not fit together very well, creating an awkward arrangement, which leaves

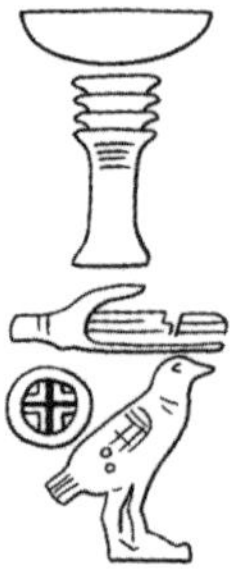

spaces in the inscription. So here the sculptor has moved ⊗ over the back of to fill up the space. Along a horizontal line we are likely to encounter a writing such as , where the determinative has moved into the middle to fill the space in .

The unexpected writings of *ꜣsỉr* and *ḏdw* introduce us to an important principle of writing, whether in hieroglyphs or in English. It is not individual signs that matter, it is combinations of signs we need to recognize. You can teach anybody which sounds are written with the letters G and H in English, but how would you then explain to them the pronunciation of 'eight' or 'enough'? In fact, even with our alphabet we learn words as distinctive groups of signs, not through their constituent letters. (How else could you learn to read and write 'eight'?) Likewise, in hieroglyphic inscriptions the combination of together alerts us to the name *ꜣsỉr*, while and with ⊗ point us to the place name *ḏdw*.

- In column 3 we have the title *ḥm-nṯr* 'priest', which is made up of two words *ḥm* 'body' and *nṯr* 'god' (hence 'god's body', a title whose meaning we can explain later, see page 105). However, the phrase seems to read with before .

The unexpected reading of leads us to another simple rule: titles that include the word *nṯr* write first, irrespective of where it is actually read in the title.

Scholars call this arrangement *honorific transposition*, which simply means that has been moved (or *transposed*) because it has special significance (it is *honoured*). This may seem odd, but you will quickly learn the correct reading of *ḥm-nṯr* in the same way that somebody learning English learns that £10 reads 'ten pounds' not 'pounds ten'. Later we will see the same rule applied to words other than *nṯr*.

No doubt your head is spinning because of these unexpected writings. However, writing is not logical nor consistent in any language: how do you explain the way we use C so differently in 'cake', 'circus', 'success' and 'cello'? Unexpected writings occur on the stela of Mereri because it is a real monument, and matters like *abbreviation* are matters you need to know about

DID YOU KNOW?

A writing such as 𓊽𓂧𓊖𓅱 *ḏdw* illustrates a crucial aspect of Egyptian hieroglyphic writing – that there was a certain amount of flexibility, which enabled artists to make the most effective use of space. The writing above may be more concise and elegant than 𓊽𓂧𓅱𓊖. On the other hand, if the space available for an inscription was very restricted, an even briefer writing of the same word would be 𓊽𓅱𓊖. Artists could vary the make-up of words, abbreviating them or spelling them out more fully, in order to make the most pleasing and varied arrangements within an inscription, whether horizontally or vertically.

in order to read ancient inscriptions. More to the point, reading hieroglyphs does not get any harder than this. Mereri's stela is real, so it has not been 'spin-doctored' to hide the difficulties from you. All you need to do now is practise what you have learned. Then practise some more. So, before you complete your reading of the stela, let us turn to our next monument: a second stela of the same man, Mereri. We can better understand what his inscriptions are about by comparing the two monuments, which we will do in **#10**. In the meantime, here is another question for you.

#9 What is Transliteration?

You have already begun thinking about the sounds of Egyptian words written both in hieroglyphs and also in a version of our own alphabet. We can write the word 𓈖 'for' as *n* because *n* is the sound written by 𓈖. Likewise, we can write 𓍿𓈖𓏏𓏏𓃒𓏥 'temple cattle' as *ṯntt* because those are its sounds. To put this another way, you can take words in hieroglyphs and write them out in a version of our own alphabet. We call this process *transliteration*, and it is good practice to get used to transliterating hieroglyphic inscriptions. Transliteration helps you to learn and remember words. Moreover, if you wish to go beyond the most basic level of reading you will eventually have to learn how to use sign lists, dictionaries, notes, etc., and Egyptologists write and organize these using transliteration. If you do transliterate inscriptions from the beginning, it will soon become second nature to you.

Because transliteration uses a form of our own alphabet, we transliterate according to our ordinary writing practice. So we transliterate in lines from left to right, whichever direction the hieroglyphic inscription is written in.

For example, we would transliterate the stela of Mereri above as follows:

ḥtp di͗ nsw ꜣsi͗r nb-ḏdw prt-ḫrw n ḥꜣty-ꜥ m-r ḥm-nṯr sꜣw ṯntt mrri͗

Here the sounds of the words are written out as we normally write, including word breaks, and we do not try to copy the columns and the right-to-left layout of the original. Also, because our own way of writing is concerned only with the sounds of words, we do not try to show the determinatives in transliteration. At first, transliteration looks peculiar because there are no vowels, and because we use special signs (*ꜣ*, *i͗*, *ꜥ*, *ḥ*, *ḫ*, *ẖ*, *š*, *ḳ*, *ṯ*, *ḏ*) for sounds that do not have their own letters in our alphabet. However, simply practise transliterating inscriptions and you will soon get familiar with it.

Now practise what you have learned:

– 1-sound, 2-sound, 3-sound signs and determinatives
– sound complements
– honorific transposition

....

....

....

....

....

....

....

....

....

Another Stela of Mereri from his Tomb at Dendereh (6th Dynasty, c. 2200 BC)

4 Another stela of Mereri, from Dendereh.
❶ An offering which the king gives Anubis / ❷ in front at the god's booth: a voice offering for / ❸ governor, overseer of priests / ❹ keeper of secrets for the god's seal bearer / ❺ Mereri
The stela was broken at the bottom right, see dotted line, and erroneously restored in modern times. The drawing opposite shows the original forms of the hieroglyphs.

Like the stela on page 10, this stela came from the tomb of Mereri at Dendereh in the south of Egypt and is now in the collections of Glasgow City Museums. They are typical of hundreds of such stelae dating from the Old Kingdom – the era of the Great Pyramid and Great Sphinx – both in Egypt and in museums around the world. Mereri is dressed in the regalia of a high official, as though to impress visitors; and this is not such a fanciful notion. His stelae were made to be a point of worship for the ritual of offering. At certain times in each month, especially during religious festivals, surviving members of Mereri's family or their representatives would visit his tomb and lay down offerings for the benefit of his soul. His soul, they believed, would outlast his time in this life. These are fundamental and unwavering ancient beliefs, which we will come back to on occasion later. For now, we can begin our exploration of these ideas by comparing the inscriptions on the two stelae.

Possibly the first thing you noticed about the second stela is that the hieroglyphs are written in lines not columns (notice how easy it is to see whether the hieroglyphs read in lines or columns). This makes an interesting visual contrast, and demonstrates the flexibility of hieroglyphic writing for decorating sacred monuments. However, it is more revealing for our present purposes to notice the similarities between the monuments. Both are rectangular, because they were decorative panels fixed into the walls of his tomb, and both are dominated by the imposing, muscular image of the man himself. In both, Mereri is shown facing right, so you begin reading on the right. In both his name has been isolated next to his body, so that the sculptor can draw your eye straight there. Finally, there are similarities in the inscriptions that are crucial for our understanding, so let us break the second stela down into individual words.

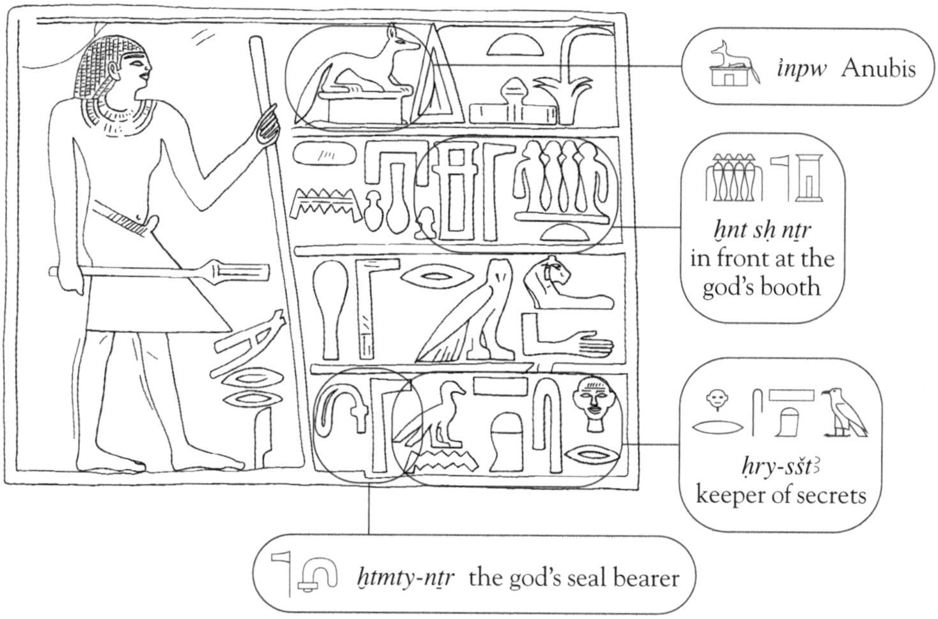

5 Second stela of Mereri with the inscription explained.

#10 What You Need to Know: The Offering Formula

If you put the words on the second stela together, you get the following transliteration and translation into English:

ḥtp dỉ nsw ỉnpw ḫnt sḥ-nṯr prt-ḫrw n ḥꜣty-ꜥ m-r ḥm-nṯr ḥry-sštꜣ n ḫtmty-nṯr mrrỉ

An offering which the king gives Anubis, in front at the god's booth: voice offering for governor, overseer of priests, keeper of secrets for the god's seal bearer, Mereri.

From the first stela you already know his name and the titles in line 3, *ḥꜣty-ꜥ* 'governor' and *m-r ḥm-nṯr* 'overseer of priests'. In line 4 you get a new title *ḥry-sštꜣ* 'keeper of secrets', which is a priestly office. (*ḥry* is abbreviated and written without *-y* at the end, as you may now expect in titles, see **#8**.) However, he is not just any 'keeper of secrets', he is 'keeper of secrets' *n ḫtmty-nṯr* 'for the god's seal bearer'.

Now, to make sense of the first two lines, compare them closely with the first two columns of Mereri's stela on page 10. You will be able to see these hieroglyphs on both:

- At the beginning of each inscription is the group *ḥtp dỉ nsw* 'an offering which the king gives'.
- At the end of the second column/line of each is the group *prt-ḫrw* 'voice offering', followed by the word *n* 'for', i.e. a voice offering for (someone).

The four hieroglyphs are perhaps the most important you are going to learn. When they appear at the beginning of an inscription, they announce that the inscription is *the offering formula*. Not surprisingly, this means the inscription is about offerings, and specifically about offerings for the benefit of

DID YOU KNOW?

You might already have noticed that Mereri had both an administrative office in Egypt (as governor) and several priestly offices (as overseer of priests, as keeper of the temple cattle and as keeper of secrets). This is entirely typical of the nation in the 3rd millennium BC, when men of the highest status served in the temples on a part-time basis, whereas the number of 'full-time' priests was small.

a dead person. The offering formula was used in Egypt from the early 3rd millennium BC until Roman rule, some 3,000 years later; it was used, among other places, on stelae, coffins, altars, offering jars, ritual objects and tomb paintings; it is, therefore, among the commonest inscriptions you may come across on hieroglyphic monuments. Moreover, because it is a formula, it imposes a standard format on the inscription. Whenever you find the offering formula you can predict much of what is going to follow, even though the details will vary from monument to monument. So let us take a closer look at the standard format, which has three parts:

1 The *introduction*, of course, is 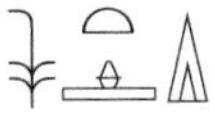 *ḥtp dỉ nsw* 'an offering which the king gives'. This is a standard phrase, usually written the same way, so this is a moment for you just to learn the group of hieroglyphs and its reading. However, you can perhaps see that it is built from the words 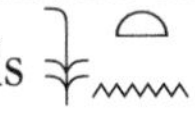 *nsw* 'king' (see **#12**) plus 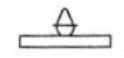 *ḥtp* 'offering' plus  *dỉ* 'give'. The king gives the offering to a god or gods. This could be any god, so there is no way to predict whose name or names will follow. None the less, you can be sure that *what follows* 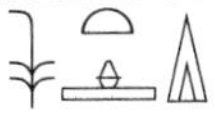 *will be the name of a god or gods*, and certain gods are most likely to appear because they are closely associated with tombs and the afterlife.

Two such gods appear on Mereri's stelae.

- On the first stela we get the introduction *ḥtp dỉ nsw ꜣsỉr nb-ḏdw* 'an offering which the king gives Osiris, lord of Djedu'.
- On the second stela we get the introduction *ḥtp dỉ nsw ỉnpw ḫnt sḥ-nṯr* 'an offering which the king gives Anubis, in front at the god's booth'.

In ancient belief, Osiris is king in the afterlife (see page 53), while Anubis is responsible for maintaining the integrity of burials. Notice that the gods are given a title as well as being named, which is also standard practice. Of course, you have to learn the names and titles of gods, but you will soon become familiar enough with Osiris and Anubis. Both are intimately connected with the afterlife, and we will meet them again more than once in this book.

2 After the introduction, there is *a statement of what is offered*. On both of Mereri's stelae this statement has been simplified to the set phrase 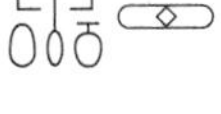

DID YOU KNOW?

According to the text, it is the king who makes the offering on Mereri's stela. It was a fundamental belief in Ancient Egyptian culture that the only mortal able to interact easily with the gods and the dead was the king. Thus, Mereri could not offer to the gods, and his family could not offer directly to Mereri, see **#19** and **#26**.

prt-ḫrw 'voice offering'. This set phrase is based on the word or *ḫrw* 'voice', which indicates that the most desirable offering for Mereri would be a spoken wish or prayer on his behalf. However, the determinatives in the phrase (foodstuffs and bread) suggest more tangible offerings of food and drink, which is an important matter we will return to later (see **#16** and **#19**). For now, Mereri cannot be displeased that you are reading the words of an offering formula on his behalf all these many centuries since his death.

3 Finally, you need to know who is going to benefit from the ritual of offering, so the offering formula has to end with *a statement of the identity of the deceased.* On Mereri's stelae, you see that the identity of an important official is explained both through his name and also through his titles. In fact, his (many) titles are so important that they go in front of his name. Obviously this part of the formula is specific to each inscription, and there is usually no way to predict what the titles and name of the deceased may be. Either you know them or you do not. However, there are a couple of points that can help here, one historical, the other practical. First, hieroglyphic monuments (other than those of kings) tend to be associated with the tombs of people at the top of what was a hierarchical society. Therefore, the people of the monuments tend to have held the same sorts of offices, and the titles they use are often the same. For example, the title *ḥꜣty-ꜥ*, 'governor' or leader of a town or community (taken literally, it means something like 'the leader in activity'), was used for more than 2,000 years in Egypt, and appears on the monuments of many men. Second, if you come across the offering formula on a monument in a museum or a book, or indeed in a tomb in Egypt, do not suppose that it is cheating to look for a museum sign or a caption, which may well tell you whose monument this was. Once you know what the sign says, you can try to find that information in the hieroglyphic inscription.

We can end this section by emphasizing the standard format of the offering formula, so take one last look at the arrangement of the inscriptions on Mereri's two stelae. On the stela on page 10, column 1 begins with the introduction *ḥtp dỉ nsw* then names Osiris, whose titles take us into column 2; column 2 ends with the statement of offerings; column 3 gives us Mereri's titles; while column 4 is his name, *mrrỉ*. On the stela on page 34, line 1 begins with the introduction *ḥtp dỉ nsw* then names Anubis, , whose titles take us into line 2; line 2 again ends with the statement of offerings; line 3 gives us Mereri's principal titles, while line 4 adds a lengthy new one; finally, line 5 is his name. In other words, you can see how the ancient craftsmen organized the layout of these inscriptions with some awareness of the three parts of the offering formula.

#11 What You Need to Know: 'a' and 'the'

In translating the second stela above, we put the title *ḫtmty-nṯr* (remember does not read first because it has undergone honorific transposition, see page 31) into English as '*the* god's seal bearer', although there is no word in the Egyptian original which is equivalent to 'the'. In Egyptian at the time of Mereri, there was no word for 'the' nor for 'a'. So, *ḫtmty-nṯr* can be put into English as 'god's seal bearer', or '*a* god's seal bearer', or '*the* god's seal bearer', as you see fit. The Egyptian original never uses such words so it will not prompt you to choose one or other translation. Likewise, you can translate *ḥꜣty-ʿ* as 'governor', or '*a* governor', or '*the* governor'. Do not be afraid to use 'a' or 'the' in translation, if you think it is required for the sake of good English.

#12 What You Need to Know: Even More Unexpected Writings

In #8 you came across unexpected writings caused by matters such as abbreviation and honorific transposition. The way to deal with these unexpected writings, if you remember, is to learn words as distinctive groups of signs rather than trying to piece them together from individual signs. Sometimes this is essential because the way a word is written seems completely at odds with the way it reads. For example, the important and very common word or 'king' (as seen in *ḥtp dỉ nsw*) is made up of the signs 𓇓 *sw* and 𓏏 *t* and 𓈖 *n*, and seems to read *swt* or *swtn*. However, you will have to take it on trust that there are good historical reasons for not believing the apparent reading (just as you do not say 'eight' the way you see it in English). A more likely reading of the group 𓇓𓏏 is *nsw*, although not all Egyptologists agree even on this. Thankfully, in Egyptian (unlike English) there are very few instances of words like *nsw*, which seem to be spelled one way, but read another.

Now practise what you have learned:

– the offering formula
– 'a' and 'the'
– the inscriptions of Mereri

#13 Ideograms?

In the second stela of Mereri, the name of the god Anubis has been written simply by drawing him as a dog lying upon a religious shrine . This is simply a way of abbreviating his name and relies on the fact that his appearance is so distinctive. If a god is simply pictured in this way and you are not sure which god is shown, often the title or titles beside his name will help. Anubis here is given the title *ḫnt sḥ nṯr* 'in front at the god's booth', and that title is all but unique to Anubis. is also an abbreviation, simply showing a booth rather than writing the sounds of the word *sḥ*. More usually, of course, an inscription will give you words written out in full, such as *inpw* or suchlike for Anubis' name.

At this point you could object that, no, must be picture writing. The sculptor meant Anubis, so he simply drew Anubis. In a sense this is true, but, remember the context in which the sculptor was working is one where most hieroglyphs write sounds, and is as common a writing of Anubis as . On the other hand, it is also true that some words always seem to rely on picture writing. For example, the word for 'mouth' is written *r*, in which the hieroglyph actually shows a mouth. The single stroke seems to have been added as though to say, this is it: you have a mouth here and that is the word you should read. Some books on hieroglyphs treat such hieroglyphs as a special category called *ideograms* – meaning signs that write what they show, especially when followed by . In truth, however, such coincidence happens too infrequently to help you much in your reading, and there seems to be little utility in talking about ideograms. Moreover, the idea that a hieroglyph written with means you should read what you see is often misleading. You already know that the word *sꜣ* is 'son' not 'duck' (see page 25). As we said right at the beginning, hieroglyphs are not intended as pictures, they are basically used to write the sounds of Egyptian. The single stroke is often combined with other signs (or) to tell you that this is not just a sign it is a whole word (*r* 'mouth' or *sꜣ* 'son'). However, does not tell you to treat the sign next to it as an ideogram. Likewise, a more effective guide to reading is to recognize that it follows the phrase *ḥtp di nsw* in the offering formula and, for that reason, ought to be the name of a god (see **#10**).

DID YOU KNOW?

Why do we not call Anubis by the name Inpu, as the hieroglyphs suggest? Why is Osiris not called Asir? Well, the names of Egyptian gods were often mentioned by Classical authors writing in Greek and Latin, so they were well known in the West long before hieroglyphs were deciphered. Most people have continued to use the familiar Classical forms, which tend to end with is, rather than their original Egyptian forms. Of course, this is partly because we cannot be sure how the original Egyptian names were pronounced (see **#3**).

None the less, you may finally object that Egyptian hieroglyphs were probably picture writing when they first started. Well, you may be surprised by the facts of the matter, and we will return to them in **#27**. For now, you have heard this before, but it bears repeating. Reading inscriptions written in Egyptian hieroglyphs *does not get any harder than this*. All the problems you are liable to encounter on hieroglyphic monuments are here on the stelae of Mereri. If you can read them, however halting your progress so far, it is time for you to move onto the next monument. This is the stela of another Old Kingdom official, Minuser, which you will meet on page 44. In the meantime, here is another question for you.

#14 What is Middle Egyptian?

Egyptian has the longest recorded history of any language – more than 4,000 years from the earliest inscriptions *c.* 3000 BC until the latest Coptic compositions of the 13th century AD. By contrast, Chinese has been written for something over 3,000 years, while written English is barely 1,500 years old. Egyptian is also the only indigenous language known from Egypt. Other languages used in the country in ancient times were imposed on the government by foreign rulers (Persian, then Greek and eventually Arabic) or introduced by settlers (including Hittite, Hurrian, Carian and Aramaic). Most languages that seem related to Egyptian – including the Berber, Cushitic, Chadic and Omotic languages of Africa – have much more recent written histories. While some of the Semitic languages of the Middle East do have long written histories, their relationship to Egyptian is not very close, especially with regard to the words they use. The ancient languages of neighbouring peoples in Nubia, Libya and the deserts are also lost to us except through a handful of personal names, such as Taharqa (Biblical *Tirhakah*), place names, such as Kush (Biblical *Cush*), and occasional loanwords in Egyptian, such as ***hbn*** (*ebony*). During the mid-1st millennium BC, Egyptian hieroglyphs were adapted to write the Nubian language Meroitic, but the language itself is unrelated to Egyptian.

Unsurprisingly, Egyptian changed enormously during the dozens of centuries in which it was written down. (Think how much English has changed in just the 600 years since Geoffrey Chaucer wrote, 'Reule wel thyself that other folk canst rede,' which means something like 'Keep control of yourself so you can be an example to others.') We noted in **#5** that the latest known phase of Egyptian is Coptic. The language in earlier periods is sometimes divided by scholars into two main phases, Earlier Egyptian from *c.* 3000 BC and Later Egyptian from the mid-16th century BC. Distinguishing these two phases are fundamental developments in the way words were used (*grammar*), the way they were written (*orthography*), and, to a lesser extent, which actual words were spoken and written (*vocabulary*). Earlier Egyptian itself can be further divided into two key phases: Old Egyptian, which means essentially the language used during the mid-3rd millennium BC; and Middle Egyptian, as used about 2200–1600 BC.

Now, Middle Egyptian is important for two reasons. On the one hand, it was a phase of the language that later generations of Egyptians considered to be especially elegant and precise, not least because many classics of Egyptian literature and religion were written in Middle Egyptian. In this sense we can compare the influence of Middle Egyptian in ancient times to the influence in our time of English around AD 1600, as used by Shakespeare, Donne or the translators of King James' Bible. On the other hand – and this is very important – Middle Egyptian continued to be used on monuments until the 4th century AD, long, long after the language people spoke (and wrote in their daily lives) had moved on to become Later Egyptian. In 2000 BC Middle Egyptian was the spoken language of Egypt, but by 1300 BC it was an archaic form used only for sacred monuments. So far, we have called the language of the inscriptions simply Egyptian, and we will continue to do so. However, you should be aware that the language of most of the monuments in this book – the language you are learning here – is actually *Middle Egyptian*.

Stela of Minuser from his Tomb, probably at Dendereh (6th Dynasty, *c.* 2200 BC)

6 Stela of Minuser, from Dendereh.
❶ An offering which the king gives Anubis, upon his hill: a voice offering for the controller of priests, Minuser / ❷ Priest, revered one, Minuser / ❸ His perfect name Wedjaw

Minuser *mnw-wsr* was a near contemporary of Mereri, and both men belonged to the same governing tier of society. His stela is now in the National Museum of Scotland, Edinburgh. Men such as Mereri would have been part of an itinerant palace community: sometimes in attendance on the king; sometimes working on delegated projects throughout the country and abroad; other times returning to their offices and homes (see page 72). Their activities bound together the government and its various communities and temples. By contrast, Minuser held his principal office in a temple, which would have put him among the leaders of his community as a point of contact for the likes of Mereri.

Obviously, Minuser's stela has much in common with those of Mereri in terms of its shape and its subject matter, although you notice immediately that there are two figures here. One of these is seated behind a table loaded with baguette-style loaves, beneath which are two jars, probably for beer and water (on the basis of what we learn in other inscriptions). Assuming that these are offerings of food and drink, the seated figure may well be the tomb owner, Minuser. The other figure stands erect and powerful in the same official's costume of kilt and collar as Mereri, with a staff and sceptre likewise. Who is he? Is he bringing the offerings, or performing some religious ceremony? Does his small size indicate that he is inferior to the tomb owner? There is much you can deduce from the images on the monument, but perhaps you need the hieroglyphic inscription to supply the missing information.

In fact, that should be hieroglyphic inscrip*tions*. If you look at the stela carefully, you notice that the hieroglyphs above the seated figure read from the right and so are aligned with him; whereas the hieroglyphs in front of the standing figure are aligned with him and read from the left. So, there are two

7 Stela of Minuser with the inscription explained.

figures and at least two inscriptions. Start at the top, with the hieroglyphs running across the stela, and you will find straight away *ḥtp dỉ nsw* 'an offering which the king gives'. Therefore, this is an offering formula, and you are able to look ahead in anticipation of what is likely to follow. For example, you can already recognize *prt-ḫrw* 'voice offering', followed by the word *n* 'for'. After *ḥtp dỉ nsw* you would expect the name of a god, and here you find Anubis again.

Between Anubis and is a title of his that you have not met before, the enigmatic *tp ḏw.f* 'upon his hill'. In fact, this is a common title for Anubis, so it would be worth your while to copy it out and remember it. As we expect, after *n* the last part of the line is going to be a statement of the identity of the tomb owner. Again, either you know his name and title or you do not. However, in this case you can see that part of his title is a phrase you know, *ḥm-nṯr* 'priest'. Unlike Mereri, he is not 'overseer of priests', he is *sḥḏ ḥm-nṯr* 'controller of priests'. All that is left at the end of the line is his name *mnw-wsr*.

Hopefully you can now see the transliteration and translation into English, something like the following:

> *ḥtp dỉ nsw ỉnpw tp ḏw.f prt-ḫrw n sḥḏ ḥm-nṯr mnw-wsr*
>
> An offering which the king gives Anubis, upon his hill: a voice offering for the controller of priests, Minuser.

The seated figure, you now know, is Minuser, and there is another text in front of his face. This text is also orientated to read from the right, so you can read it as a continuation of the top line. Here you see a new phrase *rn.f nfr* 'his perfect name' (see **#15**). A perfect name is something like the name you grow into as an adult, one which reflects the person you become. Perfect names are not uncommon on monuments of the Old Kingdom. In this case, our man has a birth name *mnw-wsr* and a perfect name *wḏꜣ-ꜣw*.

Who is the standing figure? Well, now you can probably see from the end of the inscription beside him that he is also Minuser. It is not uncommon in Ancient Egyptian art for the same man to be shown twice on the same monument, but in different aspects. Here he is both the deceased seated to receive offerings and the official standing to display his authority to visitors. The two figures have been balanced to face each other and the standing figure is drawn at a height appropriate for the space; if the standing figure were drawn in proportion to the seated figure, its head and torso would disappear off the top of the monument.

Minuser has two titles in this right-hand column: he is simply called  *ḥm-nṯr* 'priest'; and he is also called 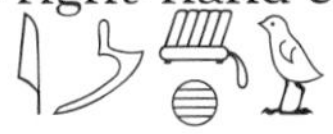 *ỉmꜣḫw*, which is a very important title to learn and be able to recognize. In effect, *ỉmꜣḫw* means somebody who is so revered as to be the subject of an offering cult. We usually translate the title as 'revered one', but the emphasis is not on Minuser's standing in his community while he was alive, rather the fact that offerings are being brought to him after death. We can read this column as *ḥm-nṯr ỉmꜣḫw mnw-wsr*, 'priest, revered one, Minuser'.

The Ancient Egyptians (other than kings) who left behind hieroglyphic monuments did so because they were *ỉmꜣḫw* and had a tomb built for them. Therefore, by definition, the people you meet in this book are *ỉmꜣḫw* and the title is liable to be applied to them on their monuments. The word itself can be written in more or less abbreviated ways, so on Minuser's stela it is written simply  without the final *-w*. However, you can usually spot it from the distinctive sign  *mꜣḫ* especially when combined with the sound complement  *ḫ* to form . Anyway, it is a title you can always keep an eye out for whenever you read an inscription from a tomb.

#15 What You Need to Know: Word Order

In Egyptian, if one word describes another word, it usually *follows the word it describes*. For example, on the stela of Minuser you have seen the phrase  *rn.f nfr* 'his perfect name'. In English, the words 'his' and 'perfect' go in front of the word they describe ('name'). In Egyptian *f* 'his' and *nfr* 'perfect' follow the word they describe (*rn*).

By the way, the word *f* 'he' or 'his' has a special characteristic: it attaches onto the end of the word it describes (in other words, it is a *suffix*). We show this special character in transliteration by writing . (stop) between *.f* and the word it attaches to, as in  *rn.f* 'his name'. Because *.f* is attached to *rn*, no other word can come between them, so *nfr* must follow after *rn.f*. Another word that behaves like *.f* and attaches onto the word it describes is 𓋴 or 𓊃 *.s* meaning 'she' or 'her'. You will see 𓋴 and 𓊃 *.s* in **#22**.

Now practise what you have learned:

– ideograms
– word order
– the inscription on the stela of Minuser

Now you have come to the point in your reading where you can start getting to know the List of Hieroglyphic Signs, which begins on page 144.

Funerary Stamp of Mermose, from his Tomb at Thebes (18th Dynasty, c. 1350 BC)

8 Inscription on the base of a cone funerary stamp of Mermose, from Thebes.
Revered one before Osiris, King's Son of Kush, Mermose.

Now that you are becoming familiar with the offering formula, it is time for you to practise reading it several times. Practice makes perfect, of course, and that is no less true here: the offering formula appears so often in tombs and on museum objects that you will quickly be able to find it and read it in many obvious locations. However, more than that, you are now going to read inscriptions from stelae and coffins, in which variations on the basic offering formula will expand your understanding about the nature of life and death in Ancient Egypt. Let us begin with a seemingly mundane object, a ceramic cone, now in Glasgow City Museums, which is far more impressive than it first appears.

We have moved forward more than 800 years into Egypt's great imperial age, the New Kingdom. Stamps on ceramic cones were sometimes slotted into the stone façades of tombs, in groups numbering up to 300, to create a frieze above or around the doorway. Although they are usually found in tombs only in the far south of Egypt, especially at Thebes, they were used there for over 800 years until the 6th century BC. One of the largest groups of stamps comes from the tomb of Mermose  *mrms*, King's Son of Kush for Amenhotep III (*c.* 1390–1353 BC). The group was dispersed among several museum collections, including this example in Glasgow City Museums.

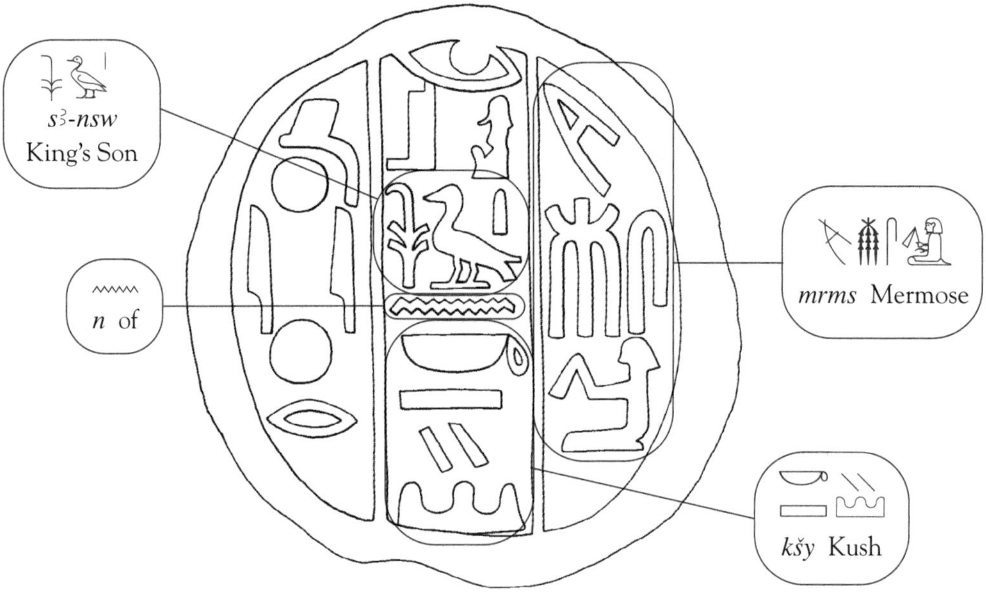

9 Cone funerary stamp of Mermose with the inscription explained.

King's Son of Kush was the title of the highest official in the Nubian lands of Wawat and Kush, occupied by Egypt from about 1550 until about 1080 BC. (Nubia is now divided between modern Egypt and Sudan.) There was only one such official at any moment and his only peers were the two viziers who occupied a comparable position within Egypt itself. As a position of utmost authority, the King's Son of Kush reported directly to the pharaoh. The delicacy and trust entailed in the office is embodied in the title itself, because neither Mermose nor most of his counterparts in this office were bodily sons of any king. Notice also that the word *nsw* 'king' (written here just as 𓇓), when it appears in titles such as 𓇓𓅭𓏤 *sꜣ-nsw*, is given *honorific transposition*. That is to say, titles that include the word 𓇓 *nsw* write 𓇓 first, irrespective of where it is actually read in the title (see page 31).

The inscription does not use the offering formula as such, but you will recognize that the language is the same. You will also notice that the title 𓄪𓐍𓇌 *imꜣḫy* is written with *-y* at the end instead of *-w*. The shift from *w* to *y* in Egyptian is only a slight (and not uncommon) change in spelling, and it makes no difference to the meaning here. Hopefully your transliteration and translation read something like the following:

imꜣḫy ḫr ꜣsir sꜣ-nsw n kšy mrms
Revered one before Osiris, King's Son of Kush, Mermose.

If you translate by adding 'a' or 'the', so much the better. For example, you may have:

A revered one before Osiris, the King's Son of Kush, Mermose.

From the inscription, it is apparent that many of the beliefs you first came across on the stelae of Mereri and Minuser are still relevant all these many centuries later, including the invocation of Osiris and the title *imꜣḫw* 'revered one'. In this case (as often elsewhere) the two ideas are linked together, so that Mermose is said to be 'a revered one' 𓐍𓂋𓊨𓁹𓀭 *ḫr ꜣsir* 'before Osiris' (see page 26). This speaks again about the belief that the tomb owner in some sense is still alive, and now in the presence of the king of the dead, Osiris.

DID YOU KNOW?

You may be wondering why we do not put Mermose's name into English as Mermes, following the convention that we add an 'e' where necessary to Egyptian words. Well, this is because Greek authors wrote other names that end with 𓄟𓋴 *-ms* as though they ended *-mosis*. A good example is 'Tuthmosis', the Greek form of the name of several kings (see page 97). Although we do not use the Greek form *-mosis*, we do take the 'o' and presume that 𓄟𓋴 *-ms* was pronounced -mose at the end of names.

Inner Coffin of Khnumhotep, from his Tomb at Deir Rifeh (12th Dynasty, c. 1800 BC)

We now travel back in time to the Middle Kingdom, an era which occupies the first quarter of the 2nd millennium BC. The coffin of Khnumhotep *ẖnmw-ḥtp*, now in the National Museum of Scotland, Edinburgh, was discovered in 1907 at Deir Rifeh in the middle of Egypt. Originally it lay within a badly decayed rectangular coffin like the one on pages 78–79. The deceased is shown with a heavy black wig, a face as golden as the sun and inlaid-stone eyes. Like Mereri and Minuser, he has a collar comprising many bands of coloured beads. However, the body of the coffin is painted like the linen-white wrappings of a mummy, with four gold strips encircling his body. Khnumhotep also wears the long false beard of the gods (as you may have noticed in the determinative). This representation of the deceased as a wrapped mummy with a bewigged and bearded face was to become a standard form for Egyptian coffins from this period until Roman rule two millennia later. The mummy-shaped coffin identifies the deceased, Khnumhotep, with Osiris. Why? *Because the followers of the pharaohs believed that they would live again after death as Osiris had done in the earliest days of this world.*

10 Coffin of Khnumhotep, son of Nebtu, from Deir Rifeh.

#16 What You Need to Know: More About the Offering Formula

Down the centre of Khnumhotep's coffin lid is a single column of gold hieroglyphs. Although this is the first coffin you have seen in the book, you may be reassured to recognize that the inscription is a standard offering formula, as follows:

ḥtp di͗ nsw ꜣsi͗r nb-ḏdw di͗.f prt-ḫrw t ḥnḳt kꜣ ꜣpd n kꜣ n m-r pr ẖnmw-ḥtp i͗r.n nbtw mꜣꜥ-ḫrw

An offering which the king gives Osiris, lord of Djedu, that he may give a voice offering of bread and beer, ox and fowl, for the spirit of the estate overseer, Khnumhotep, born of Nebtu, true of voice.

Although this is the standard offering formula, it has been elaborated in ways that became typical from the Middle Kingdom onwards. In other words, in ways that are worth learning and remembering because you may well see them on other monuments:

Did You Know?

In Egyptian mythology, when this world first took physical form, Earth (Geb) and Sky (Nut) mated to produce the first creature of this world, its king, Osiris. However, Osiris' younger brother, Seth, became ambitious to replace him. Seth eventually murdered and dismembered Osiris, who thereby became the first creature to die. Their sister, Isis, collected Osiris' remains and bound them together with linen bandages. Through her devotion and magic, he was restored to life as king in the West, and she was able to conceive his child, Horus. In time, Horus overthrew the usurper, Seth, and became king of the living. In this way, death was defeated twice over and a path to the afterlife was opened for those who followed the examples of Horus and Osiris (see **#20**). The annual festival of Osiris at Abydos was visited by worshippers from all parts of the country, who kept a vigil during the one night of the year when Osiris lay dead in his tomb. Next morning his cult statue travelled in procession back to his Great Temple amid general rejoicing. As a modern audience, we have to remember that for many ancient believers the events surrounding Osiris were real, not myths or folk-tales, while each new king was the present incarnation of Horus.

- The phrase *dỉ.f* 'that he may give' is placed in front of *prt-ḫrw*. The sense of this is quite clear: the king gives an offering to Osiris so that he (Osiris) will then give the offering to the deceased, who is in the presence of Osiris. The word *dỉ.f* is a special form of the word *rdỉ* 'give', but you do not need to know which form it is in order to make sense of the offering formula. Just learn it as part of the phrase *dỉ.f prt-ḫrw* 'that he may give a voice offering'.

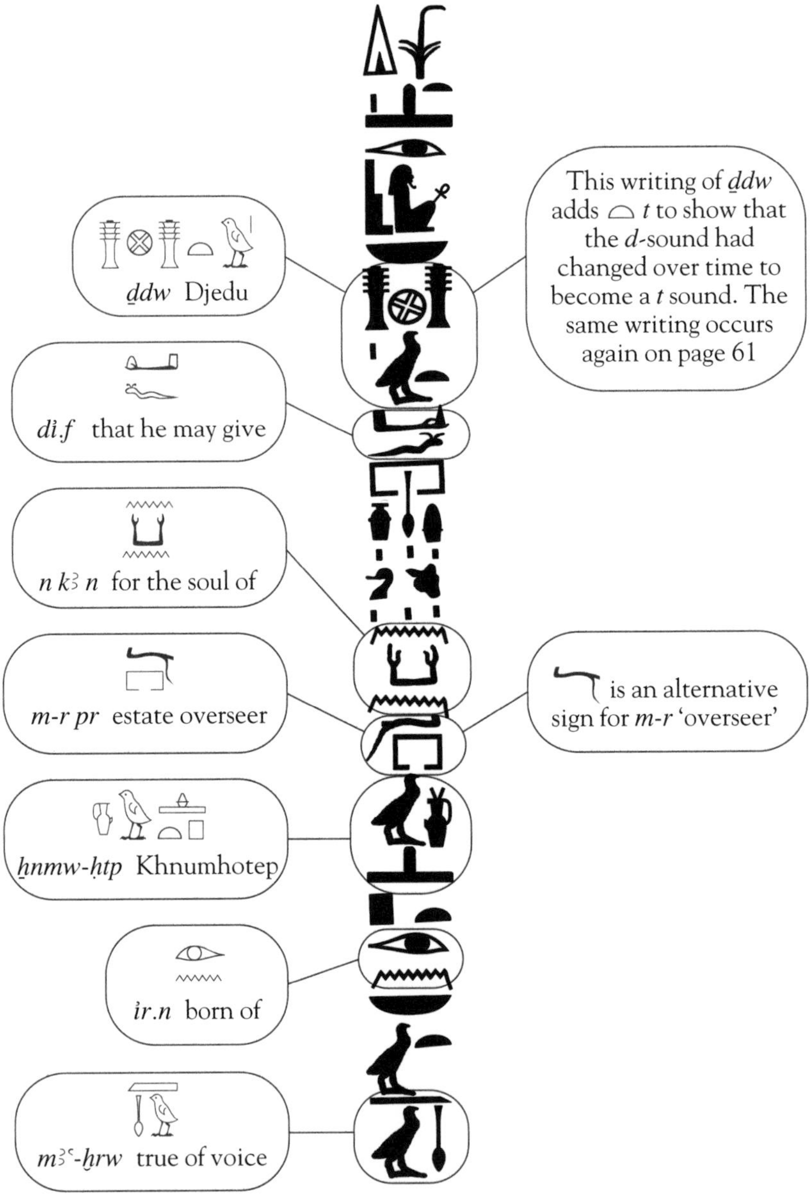

11 Coffin of Khnumhotep, son of Nebtu, with the inscription explained.

- The phrase *prt-ḫrw* itself has been elaborated by stating some of the offerings: *kꜣ* 'ox' and *ꜣpd* 'fowl' are both abbreviated as pictures of the respective animals' heads. Notice how three strokes have been added as a determinative because both words refer to a group or category of creatures, not just a single creature (see page 19). By the way, Egyptian does not usually use a word for 'and', so again this is a word you must add wherever you feel it is required for the sake of good English, hence *kꜣ ꜣpd* 'ox and fowl'.
- Now, three strokes have also been added to the group *prt-ḫrw*, and the determinative has not been written at all. Together with the appearance of *kꜣ* 'ox' and *ꜣpd* 'fowl', this may suggest that you need to understand and here not as determinatives, but as abbreviations of the words *t* 'bread' and *ḥnḳt* 'beer'. If so, we have a list of offerings that reads like this: 'a voice offering of bread and beer, ox and fowl'. Bread and beer were the basic consumable forms of the main Egyptian food crops, emmer and barley, so they are virtually representative of food and food distribution. There is often no way to be sure whether in are being used as determinatives in *prt-ḫrw* or as separate words for actual offerings. Just occasionally the words *t* and *ḥnḳt* are written out in full as part of a list of offerings, in which case we can be sure that they are meant as separate words.

#17 What You Need to Know: *kꜣ* and Identity

As you would expect, Khnumhotep's identity in the offering formula is expressed using his title and his name. The title *m-r pr* 'overseer of an estate' indicates that he was the administrator responsible for a large *pr* 'estate' with several dependent families, probably on behalf of a provincial dignitary, such as a *ḥꜣty-ꜥ* 'governor', or perhaps a large institution, such as a temple. However, on this coffin Khnumhotep's identity is elaborated in three important new ways:

- The offerings are said to be made not just *n* 'for' Khnumhotep, but *n kꜣ n* 'for the soul of' Khnumhotep (notice the two different words spelled *n* in the same phrase). This is a very useful phrase, not least because it is easier to spot than a simple . It is also very revealing about the offering cult. The Ancient Egyptian concept of the immortal soul was very sophisticated and relied on a fundamental distinction between two aspects of your identity. First is *kꜣ*, that aspect of you which engages with others – your community, your family, your colleagues and your king. In a sense, it is summarized by the offices you held in life, which itemize your contribution to your community and your king. This is why titles are so important in these inscriptions, unlike, you will have noticed, your age or the date of your death, which are never mentioned. *kꜣ* is the aspect of yourself over which you have some control in death, because by building a tomb and perhaps endowing an offering cult, you can ensure a good reputation for yourself, pass on your values and seek to fix your memory among the living long after your time here has passed. In other words, on these monuments *kꜣ* looks back to a man's engagement with this world, an engagement which is maintained after death by the offering cult. *kꜣ* is such a specifically Egyptian idea, many Egyptology books do not translate the word into English at all and simply use the anglicized form *ka* instead. The other aspect of your soul, which the ancients called *bꜣ*, we will return to on page 135.

- As well as Khnumhotep's titles you see a statement about his family or, more specifically, his parentage. He is said to be *ỉr.n* 'born of' Nebtu. This phrase is a special form based on the word *ỉrỉ* 'make' and can refer to either parent (it literally means 'whom Nebtu made'), so we cannot be sure whether Nebtu was his mother or father. A related phrase that may also appear is more specific: *ms.n* 'born of' is based on the word *msỉ* 'give birth' (and literally means 'to whom so-and-so gave birth'), so obviously must refer to the mother of the deceased. Although *ỉr.n* and *ms.n* are special forms of *ỉrỉ* and *msỉ*, you do not need to know which forms they are. Just learn them as set phrases meaning 'born of', and understand that *the name of a parent will follow.*

- The statement of identity ends with an important phrase *mꜣꜥ-ẖrw*, which literally means 'true of voice' and, like *prt-ẖrw*, is based on the word *ẖrw* 'voice'. *mꜣꜥ-ẖrw* is commonly written after a name to suggest that the deceased (and here it refers to the coffin owner, Khnumhotep, not to Nebtu) thought and spoke in accordance with the principle of Maat *mꜣꜥt*, according to which this world comes about through the will of a Creator and has meaning and purpose (see also page 90). Therefore, to think and speak according to Maat is to be in harmony with the Creator's intention. For your purposes, you would do well to learn and recognize the phrase *mꜣꜥ-ẖrw* (often abbreviated to or) because it will usually indicate *the point in front of which* the name of the deceased has been written.

Now practise what you have learned:

– the inscription on the stamp of Mermose
– the inscription on the coffin of Khnumhotep, son of Nebtu
– phrases about identity

Stela of Dedu and Satsobk from their Tomb at Thebes (12th Dynasty, c. 1900 BC)

12 Stela of Dedu and Satsobk, from Thebes.
1 Revered one before Ptah-Sokar, Dedu, born of Seni / 2 Revered one before Hathor, Satsobk, born of Nefret

The stela of Dedu  *ddw* and Satsobk  *sꜣt-sbk*, at the Metropolitan Museum of Art, New York, illustrates the basic unit of an Ancient Egyptian family: husband and wife. Although mortality rates for young people were much higher than we would tolerate, especially for women during pregnancy and childbirth, and although divorce was a straightforward process for women as well as men, the funerary art of the ancients consistently presents the ideal of a monogamous couple. However, this is the first time you have seen a woman in these monuments. Outside the royal family, holding office – and with it the wherewithal to construct your own tomb – was usually reserved for men. For women the route to high status and a funerary cult, at least as illustrated in the tombs themselves, was via marriage and, with it, clearly defined roles within the household.

On this monument the gender of each individual is distinctly apparent from their barely concealed bodies, their clothes and hairstyles, and even their respective skin colours. However, the woman, though more slender, is shown equal in height to the man and her clothes, collar and wig are as fine as his. Instead of a staff and sceptre, she carries a mirror and stands as though behind her husband; yet she embraces him as an equal. There is a sensual dimension to this scene of handsome partners in the first flowering of adulthood. (No doubt you have already begun to appreciate how the art of these funerary monuments uses images of vitality and beauty to gainsay any hint of morbidity or decay within the tomb.)

The woman's apparent equality within the partnership extends to the inscriptions, where one line refers to the man and the other to the woman. We can transliterate and translate the lines into English as follows:

❶ *ỉmꜣḫw ḫr ptḥ-skr ddw ms.n snỉ*
Revered one before Ptah-Sokar, Dedu, born of Seni.

Ptah-Sokar is an evocative union of the Creator, named Ptah at the great community of Memphis, with Sokar, a god of the Memphis cemetery. In this way, birth and death are united as two aspects of the same process, each entailing the other. As each new life must eventually end, so each death may end in life. By the way, notice how both gods' names have simply been written with 1-sound signs and no determinatives.

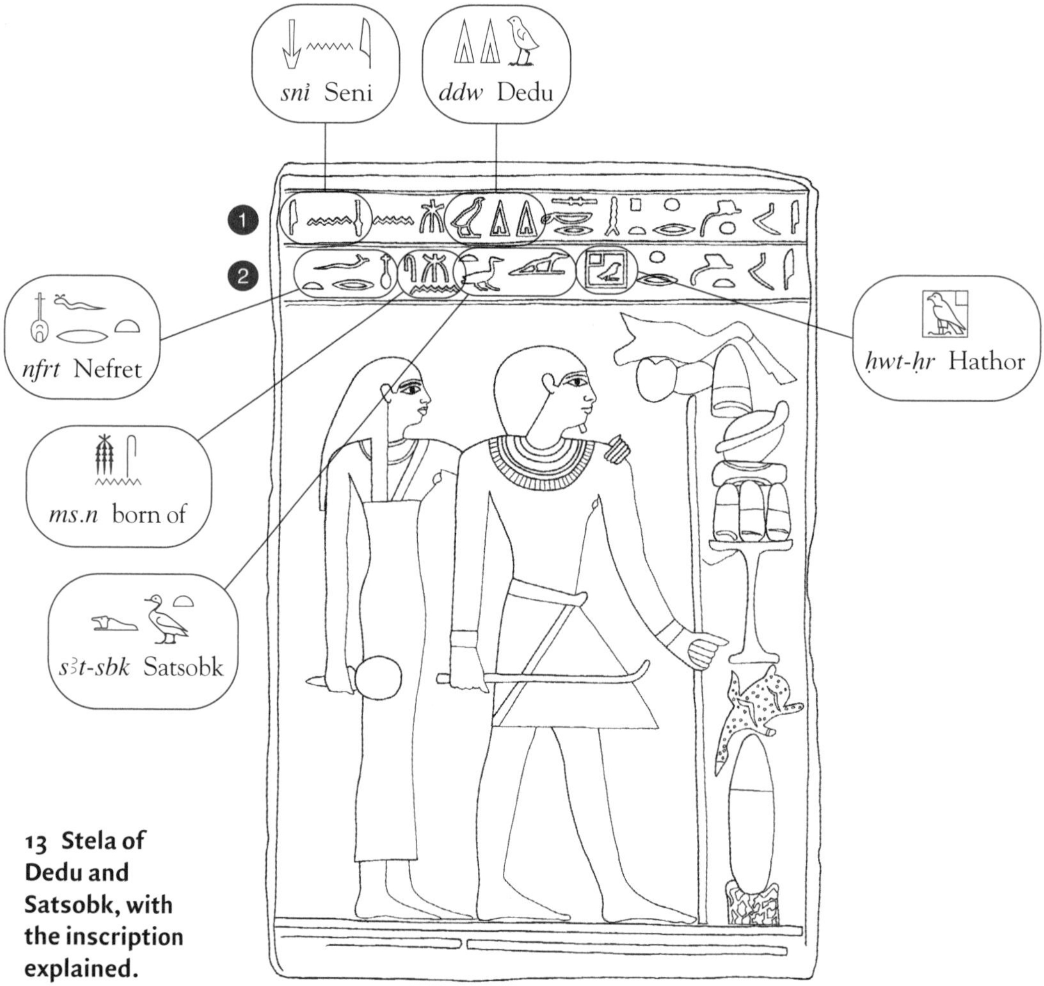

13 Stela of Dedu and Satsobk, with the inscription explained.

2 *ỉmꜣḫt ḥr ḥwt-ḥr sꜣt-sbk ms.n nfrt*
Revered one before Hathor, Satsobk, born of Nefret.

From the second line you learn that Satsobk, like her husband, has the status of 'revered one', and by this status is associated with Hathor, who was a goddess as well as a wife and mother. The mirror was well known as a symbol associated with the worship of Hathor, so you may understand Satsobk's mirror as a symbol of her spiritual condition as a woman, rather than a shallow reference to vanity. As a final note, her name *sꜣt-sbk* (which means 'daughter of Sobk') has been written with honorific transposition (see page 31), so that the name of the god *sbk* is written first, even though we know to read it last (see also page 31).

DID YOU KNOW?

The formality of Ancient Egyptian funerary art starts by locating figures on a horizontal baseline, with other lines parallel or at right angles to the baseline. Human figures are divided into simple proportions and sketched as composites, often indistinguishable in age, but the results are both handsome and elegant. For example, with shoulders shown from the front, torsos seem very slender because they are in profile with no hips. Eyes seen in full are large and attractive set in profile faces. The formality of funerary art upheld established principles, first among which was to be truthful: Egyptian artists considered observations such as perspective or emotion to be momentary distortions. Scenes conveyed timeless facts, such as status, authority and eminence. High officials have noble features and powerful bodies, adorned only with symbols of office and a kilt for modesty. Their beautiful wives seem naked, with only straps and hemlines to suggest their clothing. Such compositions were so successful they became part of every artist's repertoire for centuries and, at its worst, the art of the tombs of Ancient Egypt can be mechanical. However, in talented hands, funerary art is an attractive and inspiring style, which can express abstract and profound ideas concisely and in recognizably human terms.

#18 What You Need to Know: Feminine Words

Look carefully at the two lines of the inscription, and you will see that Dedu is described as  *ỉmꜣḫw* (without the *-w* written, like on the stela of Minuser, see page 45), but Satsobk is said to be  *ỉmꜣḫt*, with a  *t*. Now, what is this  *t* doing? In Egyptian, all words are treated as though they are masculine or feminine, whether or not they refer to things that belong to either sex. For example, the word  *t* 'bread' is masculine and the word  *ḥnḳt* 'beer' is feminine, although neither can be said to belong to either sex. This is a matter of language, not of biology, and it leads to a simple rule:

- If a word describes another word that is feminine, then the word that describes it must also become feminine. It does this by adding final  *t*.

Now, it so happens that the name Satsobk must be feminine (for reasons of biology as well as language), so to describe her name  *ỉmꜣḫw* must add  *t* at the end and become  *ỉmꜣḫt* (not *ỉmꜣḫwt* because the weak sound *-w* disappears, see page 13). As you can see from the inscriptions above, the change at the end does not affect the meaning at all, it just shows you that  *ỉmꜣḫt* belongs with  *sꜣt-sbk*. When a word changes its ending to show that it is describing another word, we call the change *agreement*.

By the way, the rule above does not say that all feminine words end in 𓏏 *t* (nor that all words ending in *-t* are feminine). It only says that *words that describe feminine words* must add 𓏏 at the end. For example, the inscriptions on these stelae name two mothers, whose names must be feminine words:

- Satsobk's mother is named 𓄤𓆑𓂋𓏏 *nfrt*, which has 𓏏 at the end.
- However, Dedu's mother is named 𓋴𓈖𓇋 *snỉ*, which does not.

#19 Why Food Offerings?

Once again you see a table filled with offerings in front of the deceased, Dedu and Satsobk. Following the conventions of funerary art, the offerings are shown individually and without interference, so they seem to rise in an unlikely column, in defiance of gravity, to show cuts of beef, onions, bread, roast fowl and a jar of beer at bottom. Why did the Ancient Egyptians place so much emphasis on offering food and drink to the souls of the dead? Of course, it is difficult to provide a full and comprehensive explanation of the religious practices of any culture, but there are certainly three aspects of the act of offering food and drink, which you need to be aware of:

- Food and drink were offered in the temples of every god in Egypt, partly as an act of thanksgiving for the bounty that the gods supply. By offering food and drink to ancestors the dead were identified with the gods. This is in accordance with the belief that death involves a transition from 'living' to *dwꜣt*, written 𓇼𓏏𓉐 or 𓇽, the condition in which the gods exist. Literally 𓇼𓏏𓉐 *dwꜣt* means 'state of adoration', and offerings are a way to 'adore' the dead just as effectively as the gods. Offerings for all the gods were provided to the temples by the king, and likewise the ubiquitous phrase 𓇓𓏏𓊵𓏙 *ḥtp dỉ nsw* tells you that it was the king who allowed offerings for the souls of all the dead.

- The basic Egyptian word for 'food' or 'sustenance' is 𓂓𓏏𓏥 *kꜣw*, which can be associated by word play with 𓂓 *kꜣ*, the aspect of the soul that is foremost in the offering formula (see **#17**). In this case, the word play suggests that offerings can actually sustain a soul. Of course, among the offerings could well be 𓃒 'ox', which is another word with the sound *kꜣ*.

- On a more straightforward level, family members (or their representatives) taking food and drink to a tomb during festivals would be able to share a meal in the presence of their ancestors. The souls of the deceased would be present among them, at least by implication, and the continuity of the family was maintained despite the physical removal of important members. Texts which modern scholars call 'letters to the dead' leave no doubt that some Ancient Egyptians at least believed it was possible to make direct contact with the souls of the dead through the act of offering food and drink.

Now practise what you have learned:

– the inscription of Dedu and Satsobk

– feminine words

....

....

....

....

....

....

....

....

....

....

Stela of Ty from his Tomb at Dendereh (?) (6th Dynasty, *c.* 2200 BC)

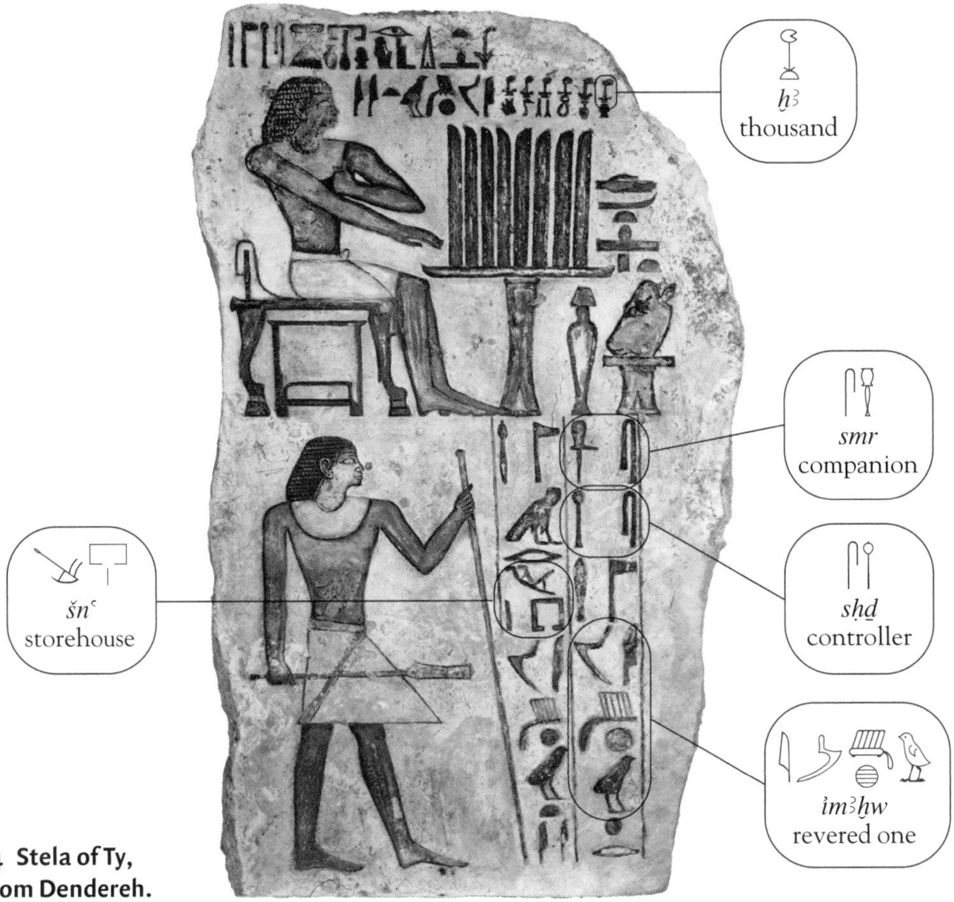

14 Stela of Ty, from Dendereh.

The stela of Ty *ty*, at the National Museum of Scotland, Edinburgh, is very similar to that of Minuser in date and arrangement (see page 44), although Ty's stela is organized vertically rather than horizontally. The upper scene shows Ty sat at a table of offerings, above which you will find an interesting new detail: a list of offerings in which each item is preceded by the word *ḫꜣ* 'thousand'. In this list you can recognize *t ḥnḳt* 'bread and beer', plus *ꜣpd kꜣ* 'fowl and ox'. Between them are two new words, *šs* 'alabaster' and *mnḫt* 'linen', which invoke the materials used for funerary jars, embalming and the general preparation for burial. Together the list gives a fairly full statement of the offerings that may be brought to the tomb:

ḫꜣ t ḫꜣ ḥnḳt ḫꜣ šs ḫꜣ mnḫt ḫꜣ ꜣpd ḫꜣ kꜣ

1000 bread, 1000 beer, 1000 alabaster, 1000 linen, 1000 fowl, 1000 ox

Next to the offering table another new phrase captions and summarizes what you can see here: *dbḥt ḥtp* literally means 'asked-for offerings', based on the words *dbḥ* 'ask for' and *ḥtp* 'offering' (see **#10**). *dbḥt ḥtp* frequently appears in this way as a label for the whole scene. Of course, the implication is that you are looking at the offerings 'asked for' by saying *prt-ḫrw* 'a voice offering'.

Above and beside the list of 'thousands' is the offering formula itself:

ḥtp dỉ nsw ꜣsỉr prt-ḫrw n sḥḏ ḥm-nṯr ỉmꜣḫw ty

An offering which the king gives Osiris: a voice offering for the controller of priests, revered one, Ty.

You may be tempted to read the list of 'thousands' as part of this offering formula, but, if the two were a single inscription, the list would appear awkwardly between *sḥḏ ḥm-nṯr* 'controller of priests' and *ỉmꜣḫw* 'revered one', in the middle of Ty's titles, so it must be a separate inscription rather than part of the formula.

The lower scene shows the official in his full regalia while elaborating on his titles:

smr sḥḏ ḥm-nṯr ỉmꜣḫw ḫr nṯr ʿꜣ m-r šnʿ ỉmꜣḫw ty

Companion, controller of priests, revered one before the great god, overseer of a storehouse, revered one, Ty.

According to this, Ty holds titles in three areas of the administration of his land (see page 36). The title *smr* 'companion' associates him with the king at the palace; the title *sḥḏ ḥm-nṯr* 'controller of priests' associates him with his local temple; while the title *m-r šnʿ* 'overseer of a storehouse' identifies him in his own community as a man who can provide grain, which may be vital for others in times of hardship. By the way, the *nṯr ʿꜣ* 'great god' is Osiris (see **#20**).

Stela of Intef and Nesumontju from a Tomb at Thebes (mid-2nd millennium, c. 1700 BC?)

15 Stela of Intef and Nesumontju, from Thebes.

The stela of Intef *intf* and Nesumontju *n-sw-mnṯw*, discovered by the Metropolitan Museum of Art, New York, in 1916, is inscribed with an offering formula for the benefit of two men. The relationship between them is not clear. They have different mothers, but did they perhaps have the same father? Serial monogamy, caused by the death of a husband or wife was far from uncommon in the ancient world. On the other hand, there are communal monuments from Ancient Egypt that group together men with a common occupation, so were Intef and Nesumontju work colleagues?

Whatever the explanation may be, their monument brings together phrases and formulas you already know. Do not be daunted by the length of the inscription: it is just made up of lots that you already know. So, see how well you can read the inscription using the words given to you above, but maybe without the help of the transliteration and translation below.

ḥtp dỉ nsw ꜣsỉr nb-ḏdw ḫnty-ỉmntw nb-ꜣbḏw
An offering which the king gives Osiris, lord of Djedu, foremost of the westerners, lord of Abydos:

prt-ḫrw t ḥnḳt kꜣ ꜣpd n ỉmꜣḫw ỉntf ms.n snỉ
a voice-offering of bread and beer, ox and fowl, for the revered one, Intef, born of Seni;

ḫꜣ t ḥnḳt kꜣ ꜣpd n ỉmꜣḫw ḫr nṯr ꜥꜣ nb-pt n-sw-mnṯw ms.n ỉy
1000 bread and beer, ox and fowl, for the revered one before the great god and lord of the sky, Nesumontju, born of Ay.

#20 What You Need to Know: Titles of Osiris

On this monument you see quite a long statement of the titles and authority of Osiris (see page 53). You already know him as  *nb-ḏdw* 'lord of Djedu', but here he is also 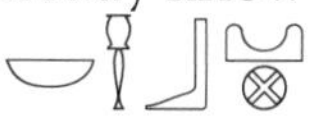 *nb-ꜣbḏw* 'lord of Abydos'. Djedu and Abydos were the major centres for the worship of Osiris, and, indeed, his sacred tomb, from the beginning of time, was believed to be situated in the desert west of Abydos. You also know Osiris as king of the dead, and here he is given his typical title  *ḫnty-ỉmntw* 'foremost of the westerners'; 'the westerners' are the dead who have passed into the realm where the sun sets. On Intef's side of the stela, the titles of Osiris talk about him with regard to worldly locations. However, Nesumontju is said to be  *ỉmꜣḫw ḫr* 'revered one before'  *nṯr ꜥꜣ* 'the great god' and  *nb-pt* 'lord of the sky'. The titles on this side of the stela also belong to Osiris, but they talk about him in transcendent language as an immanent god of creation.

Stela of Shenwy and Hedjret from a Tomb at Abydos (12th Dynasty, *c.* 1900 BC)

16 Stela of Shenwy and Hedjret, from Abydos.

The stela of Shenwy *šnwy* and Hedjret *ḥḏrt*, in the Petrie Museum of Egyptian Archaeology, London, has the longest inscription you have been asked to read. Never fear, because there is much here you will recognize, if you take the inscription step by step. In addition, there are interesting new phrases, which you are liable to find on other monuments, and the inscription looks back to things you have learned already about the offering cult, the *pr* 'estate' (page 55) and the family (pages 59–60). Finally, you may be intrigued to read what seems to be the earliest written record of the name Jesus.

Whenever an inscription seems long and complex, begin with what you know. The image at the bottom shows you that this is an offering scene based around a man and woman. So why not look for the offering formula *ḥtp dỉ nsw*? Here you find two examples: at ❶ and at ❷. Already you may feel more comfortable about what lies ahead. So begin with ❶ and scan ahead to find standard elements of the offering formula.

- You know Osiris and his titles (see **#20**).
- You know the phrase *prt-ḫrw* 'voice offering', as well as a list of offerings including *t ḥnḳt* 'bread and beer', *kꜣ ꜣpd* 'ox and fowl', and *šs mnḫt* 'alabaster and linen' (see page 64).
- You know the phrase *n kꜣ n* 'for the soul of' and the epithet *ỉmꜣḫw*.
- At the end of line 2 *mꜣꜥ-ḫrw* is a phrase you know: 'true of voice'.

In fact, there are only a couple of gaps to fill in, and you know roughly what they must be about because of where they appear in the formula: **A** must be about offerings; while **B** must be somebody's identity. See how much of this 'challenging' inscription you can read without any new knowledge? Now, to take the gaps in turn:

- **A** is filled by a common (so worth memorizing) summary of the list of offerings:

  ḫt nbt ꜥnḫt nṯr ỉm
  'everything which a god lives on'.

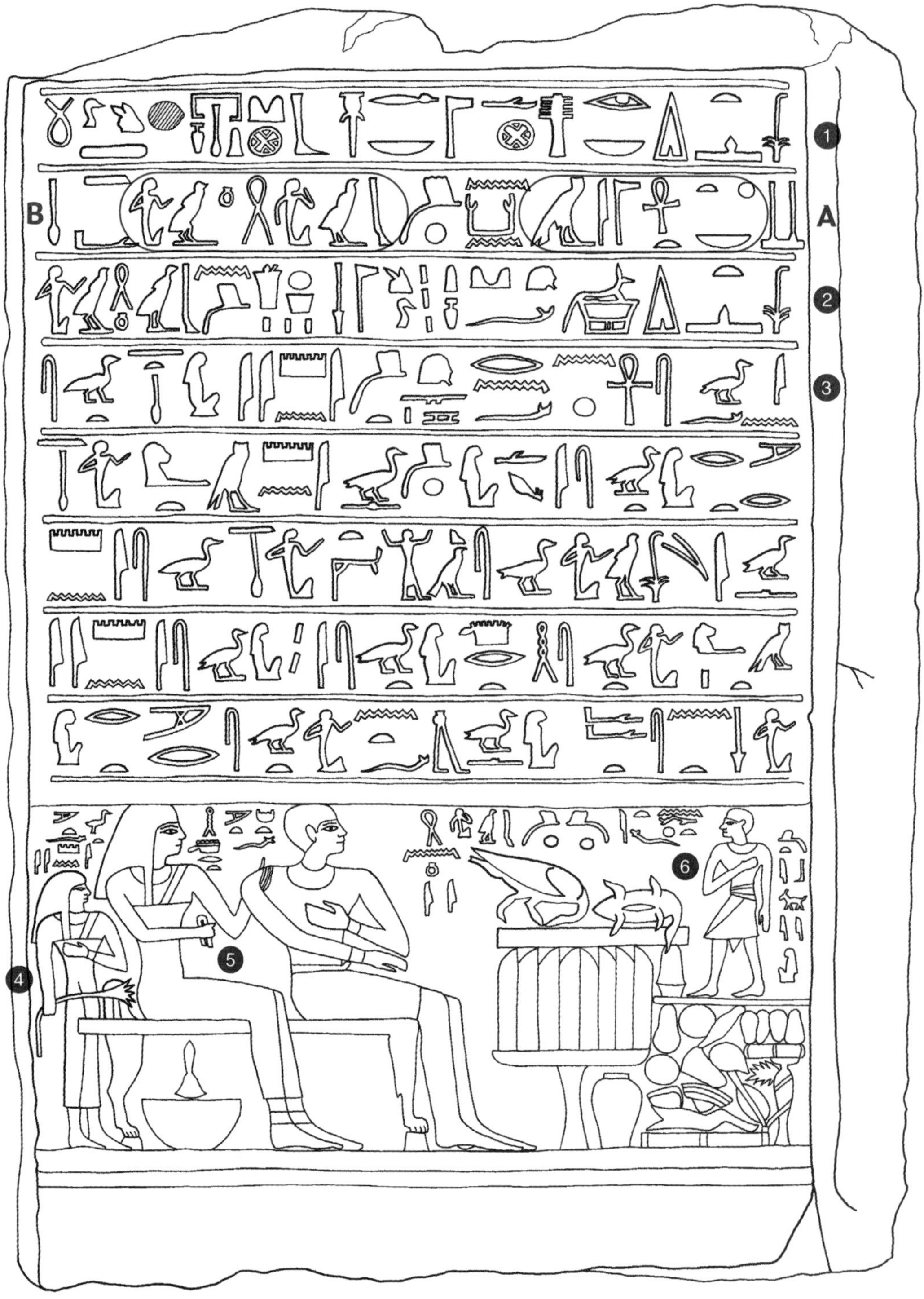

17 Stela of Shenwy and Hedjret with the sections marked.

The key words here are *ḫt nbt* 'every thing' plus the words *ꜥnḫ* 'live' and *nṯr* 'god' which you already know (see page 31). The phrase *ꜥnḫt nṯr ỉm* 'which a god lives on' uses special forms (e.g. *ꜥnḫt*) you need not worry about. Simply learn this as a set phrase. In fact, two other words you know – *nfr* 'perfect' and *wꜥb* 'pure' – are often added to create the longer, very common, formula: *ḫt nbt nfrt wꜥbt ꜥnḫt nṯr ỉm* 'everything *perfect and pure* which a god lives on'. Remember because *ḫt* 'thing' is a feminine word, all the words which describe it must have a final *-t* (*nbt, nfrt, wꜥbt*, see **#18**).

- **B** ends with the epithet 'true of voice', which often follows names. So look ahead of it for a name you know. Sure enough, there you find *šnwy* 'Shenwy', a little abbreviated, but otherwise the name given to you at the beginning of this section (or perhaps, had you not got this book to hand, you could have taken it from the label in the museum). All that is left now is to find his title, and, in the usual way, either you know *wḥmw* 'messenger' or you do not. Well, you know *wḥmw* now.

Hopefully you have this reading for lines **1** and **2**:

ḥtp dỉ nsw ꜣsỉr nb-ḏdw nṯr ꜥꜣ nb-ꜣbḏw
prt-ḫrw t ḥnḳt kꜣ ꜣpd šs mnḫt ḫt nbt ꜥnḫt nṯr ỉm
n kꜣ n ỉmꜣḫw wḥmw šnwy mꜣꜥ-ḫrw

An offering which the king gives Osiris, lord of Djedu, great god, lord of Abydos:
a voice offering of bread and beer, ox and fowl, alabaster and linen, everything which a god lives on,
for the soul of the revered one, the Messenger, Shenwy, true of voice.

Now, take your new-found knowledge to the scene at the bottom and the important man seated at the offering table. Not surprisingly, you can read in front of him:

ỉmꜣḫw wḥmw šnwy 'the revered one, the Messenger, Shenwy'.

DID YOU KNOW?

Perhaps you have asked yourself why a 'Messenger' should be so important as to deserve such an impressive monument? Well, you would be wrong to think of Shenwy as a postman or courier. He was one of those trusted officials who oiled the administrative wheel of pharaonic Egypt by carrying information between local governors, major institutions and, very likely, the palace itself. This brought him not only close to the centres of power, but also into the world of writing, which was restricted to very few in Ancient Egypt. The mix of power and literacy in life has allowed Shenwy and his family to take their places, each as an  *im3ḫw* 'revered one', in death.

Now for offering formula ❷. You probably see immediately that the god mentioned here is Anubis, with his usual title 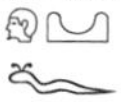 *tp ḏw.f* 'upon his hill' (see page 45). Then a list of offerings, including a new pair for you: 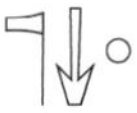 *sntr* 'incense' and  *mrḥt* 'ointment'. (Here, as often, they are written as a group  with determinatives between them.) Finally, you know Shenwy and his titles, so you can read:

> *ḥtp di nsw inpw tp ḏw.f*
> *t ḥnḳt k3 3pd sntr mrḥt*
> *n im3ḫw wḥmw šnwy*
> An offering which the king gives Anubis, upon his hill:
> bread and beer, ox and fowl, incense and ointment,
> for the revered one, the Messenger, Shenwy.

So far so good, but there are still five more lines to go. Again, this is not something that should worry you, because they essentially consist of a list of the names of Shenwy's family. In order to follow the rest of the inscription works, let us take it in two parts below, **#21** and **#22**.

#21 What You Need to Know: The Dedication Formula

At ❸ is another formula for you to commit to memory. Once you have done so, you can find this formula elsewhere and it always points out important information. It usually appears as you see it here on the stela:

 *in s3.f sꜥnḫ rn.f tp t3*

It is his son who has kept alive his name on earth.

Again, this formula uses special forms of words, but the important ideas are clear enough. The principal actor in the formula is not a king or a god, or even Shenwy himself: the subject is *sꜣ.f* 'his son' and he has done something for Shenwy or specifically for *rn.f* 'his name'. The group *ỉn* points out the subject. What he has done is *sꜥnḫ*, 'keep alive', which is obviously related to *ꜥnḫ* 'live'. The idea of a son keeping his father's name alive *tp tꜣ* 'on earth' is as meaningful in English as in Egyptian. How does a son do this? Perhaps, as here, by having a monument carved for his father's tomb or for a sacred precinct, a practice not far removed from the one we see in our own cemeteries and places of worship.

Amid the exotic beliefs of the ancients, it is reassuring to find a practice with which we can identify. Moreover, for you as a reader of hieroglyphs another benefit of recognizing the formula *ỉn sꜣ.f sꜥnḫ rn.f* is that it identifies family members, so it will usually be followed by a name or names. However, just when you think you are on familiar ground, in this monument a couple of twists are lurking.

#22 The Family

The name that follows the dedication formula is *ỉmny* 'Ameny'. So is this the son who has made the dedication? Well, look more closely. Before the name is the epithet *ỉmꜣḫt* 'revered one', and after the name is the epithet *mꜣꜥt-ḫrw* 'true of voice'. What do these epithets tell us? First, these are funerary epithets, so Ameny is dead also (or, rather, was when this stela was carved). Secondly, the agreement ending *-t* for each epithet indicates that Ameny was female (see **#18**). Look to the bottom, to the scene of Shenwy at the table of offerings. You may presume the woman seated beside him is his wife because that is the norm in funerary art (see page 59), but behind them both is another figure at ❹. She is described as *sꜣt.f mrt ỉmny* 'his beloved daughter, Ameny' (for *mry* 'beloved', see page 99). Undoubtedly, Ameny in the dedication formula is the dead woman (or girl) shown at the funerary table.

Could a dead woman be 'his son' of the dedication formula? Yes, perhaps, in the sense that anybody who makes such a dedication would be acting like 'his son' might be expected to do. If this applies to Ameny, then presumably she did commission the stela, but died while it was being carved. For Ameny to be the dedicator is much less tricky than to suggest that 'his son' refers to somebody else, altogether unnamed.

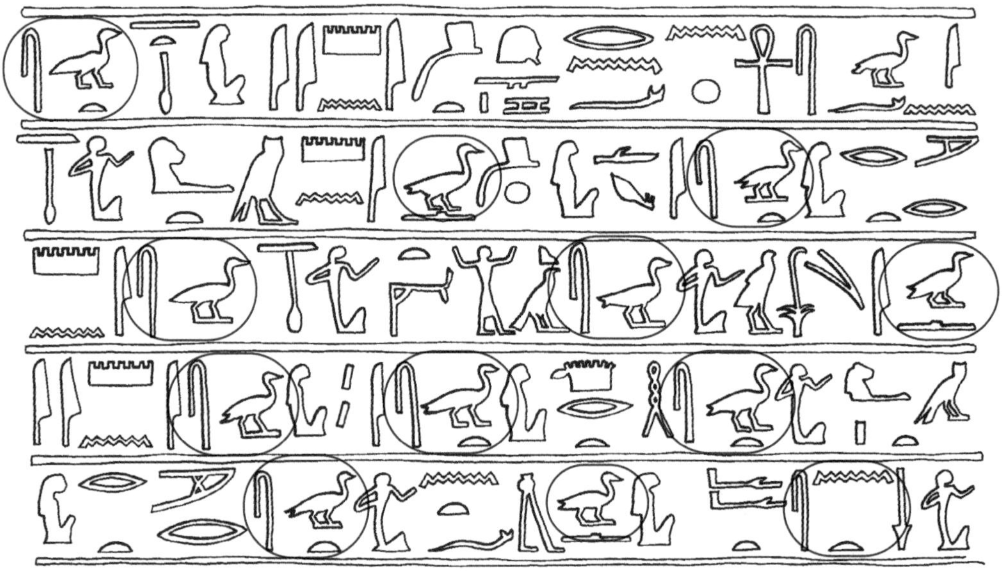

18 The list of family members with the locations of the words *s3.s*, *s3t.s* and *snt.s* circled.

Perhaps the least convoluted explanation is that the formula 'it is his son who has kept alive his name' does introduce the dedicator, and is such a standard form of words it does not need to be changed. However, here is the next twist. In this case the dedicator (the 'son') is not only Ameny, it is Ameny and the whole list of people named afterwards.

In order to divide up the list you have to identify two recurrent phrases: *sꜣ.s* 'her son' and its female counterpart *sꜣt.s* 'her daughter' (see the detail above). In other words, the dedication is made by Ameny and *her* children. The only exception is a reference to *snt.s* 'her sister' followed by the sister's children. Look at the list and you see it divides up as follows:

It is his son who has kept alive his name on earth.

Revered one, *ỉmny* 'Ameny', true of voice.

Her daughter *mrrt* 'Mereret'.

Her daughter *ỉdn* 'Iden'.

Revered one, her son *ỉmn-m-ḥꜣt* 'Amenemhat', true of voice.

Her son *ỉsw* 'Yesu'.

Her son *ḳꜣỉt* 'Qait', true of voice.

Her son *ỉmn-m-ḥꜣt* 'Amenemhat'.

Her daughter *ḥḏrt* 'Hedjret'.

Her daughter *ỉy* 'Iy'.

Her son *ỉmny* 'Ameny'.

Her sister *ddt* 'Dedet'.

Her son *ỉntf* 'Intef'.

Her daughter *mrrt* 'Mereret'.

This can hardly be a genealogy (in the sense that each person is the child of the previous person) because 12 generations make no sense in the context of the offering cult (see **#10**). These people are part of the immediate family, which includes Shenwy and his daughters Ameny and 'her sister' Dedet. Dedet has a son and a daughter. Ameny apparently has four daughters and five sons, two of whom are also dead at this time (indicated by the use of 'revered one' and 'true of voice'). Of course, you may read the list in such a way that some of Ameny's 'children' are actually children of children, who can be sure? In Egyptian there are no words for grandchild or grandparent, only words for brother and sister (*sn* and *snt*), father and mother (*ỉt* and *mwt*), and son and daughter (*sꜣ* and *sꜣt*).

Now, look back to the scene at the bottom of the stela. At ❺, beside the woman who would seem to be Shenwy's wife, you can indeed read *ḥmt.f mrt ḥḏrt* 'his beloved wife, Hedjret'. You can add another generation to this family by looking to the inscription at ❻, where you meet *ỉt.f nḫt* 'his father, Nakht'. Behind the figure of Nakht is a column of hieroglyphs that read *ỉmꜣḫt ỉby* 'revered one, Iby'. The epithet *ỉmꜣḫt* and the determinative tell you Iby is a woman, presumably the wife of Nakht. Therefore, you now have the beginning of a family tree:

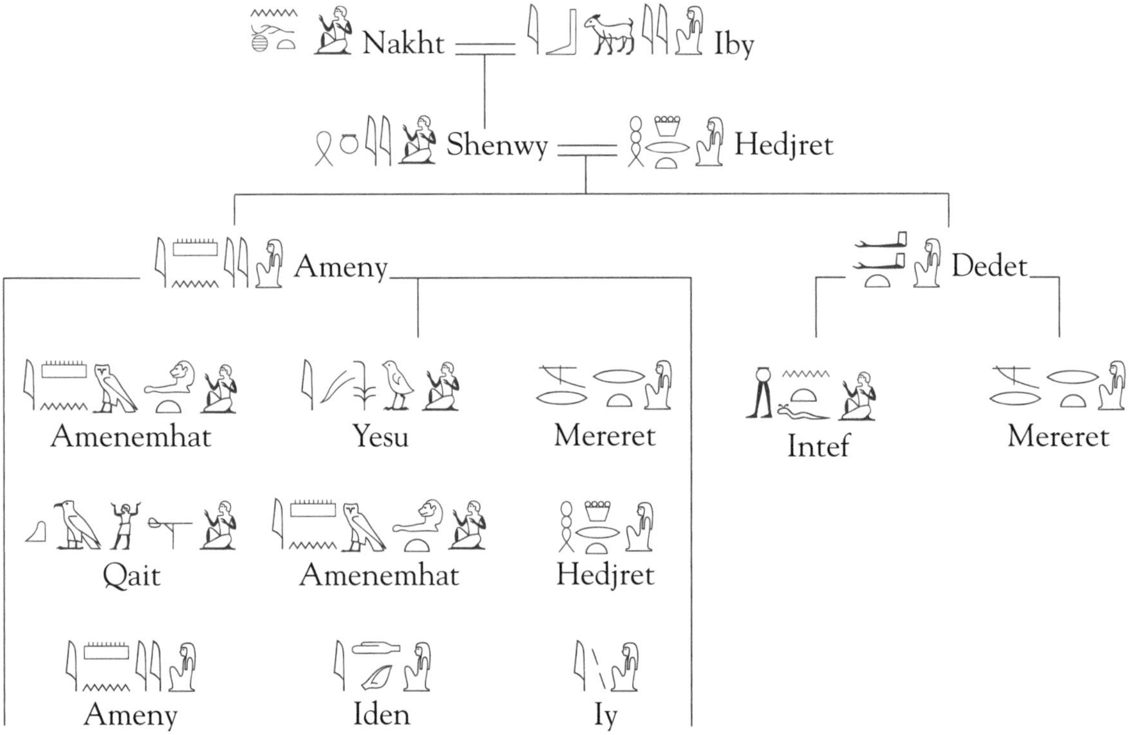

The stela shows you how the offering cult holds this family together, even after the loss of key members. Of course, it also reveals how death does not respect generations. Ameny apparently lost two children, perhaps naming a second son Amenemhat following the death of a previous son by that name, who appears earlier in the list. Indeed, one explanation for the appearance of Ameny in death as the principal dedicator of this monument is that she died around the same time as her father. Such tragic coincidences would not have been uncommon when, for example, nobody understood how to use antibiotics to treat contagious diseases.

At last you have it: a long inscription, but one you can read, and from it learn much about life and death in Ancient Egypt. There is a final point of interest: among these people are some non-Egyptian names, including the name of Shenwy's wife, Hedjret  *ḥḏrt*, which seems to be derived from a Semitic language, such as Canaanite. Of course, her name does not mean she herself was foreign, and her grandchildren have a mix of Egyptian and non-Egyptian names. However, there are many historical records of undoubted foreigners settling in Egypt and pursuing lives among the ruling group. This fact must be set against the Biblical image of Egypt under the pharaohs as a land where foreigners were typically enslaved. Instead, another Biblical reference stands out on this stela. One of Hedjret's grandsons is called  *ỉsw*, which may be the earliest historical record of the Semitic name Jesus (Hebrew ישוע = *ỉšw*).

Now practise what you have learned:

– the inscription on the stela of Shenwy and Hedjret
– the dedication formula
– family relationships

Coffin of Khnumhotep, Son of Henib, from his Tomb at Cusae (12th Dynasty, *c.* 1850 BC)

Now that you have read an inscription as long as the stela of Shenwy and Hedjret, there is not much that should concern you going forward in your study of hieroglyphs. However, before we leave the offering formula, there is a useful skill for you to practise: one that depends upon the confidence you have gained so far. Whether in museums or in excavations, Egyptologists are liable to come across objects on which the ancient inscriptions have been damaged, obscured or partly lost. None the less, often the inscriptions can confidently be read because what is left is a recognizable formula. Here you can practise this skill on a coffin in the National Museum of Scotland, Edinburgh.

This is the coffin of a priest called *ẖnmw-ḥtp* 'Khnumhotep', although he is not the same man whose coffin you looked at on page 52. It is made of wood, washed with plaster, then painted yellow with blue hieroglyphs. Excavated amid the debris of a looted cemetery in 1914, the coffin did not reach its present home for 65 more years, so you can imagine how the delicate construction might have suffered even in recent decades. Can the inscriptions still be read?

Khnumhotep's mummy was laid on his left side so his face rested behind the eyes on one side of the coffin. Vertical bands describe him as *ỉmꜣḫy ḫr* 'revered one before', then the name of a god (see page 51). The better-preserved bands at the foot name the goddess *tfnwt* 'Tefnut' and the god *dwꜣmwtf* 'Duamutef'.

A longer inscription runs along the upper margin (copied in the box over the page), but the beginning has obviously been lost. What do you see after this lost beginning? (A) Titles of Osiris. (B) A list of offerings (see pages 64–65). (C) The summary phrase *ḫt nbt nfrt wꜥbt ꜥnḫt nṯr ỉm* 'everything perfect and pure which a god lives on' (see pages 69–71). (D) The epithet *n ỉmꜣḫw* 'for the revered one', with the name *ḫnmw-ḥtp*. In fact, the only word you have not seen before is Khnumhotep's title *wꜥb* 'priest' (literally 'pure one'). Obviously the inscription is an offering formula, so the lost beginning must be *ḥtp dỉ nsw*, followed by the name *ꜣsỉr* and, you may assume, the god's most common title, *nb-ḏdw* 'lord of Djedu'.

You see how familiarity with the offering formula not only allows you confidence when reading inscriptions, but confidence when making sense of

19 The coffin of Khnumhotep, son of Henib, from Cusae.

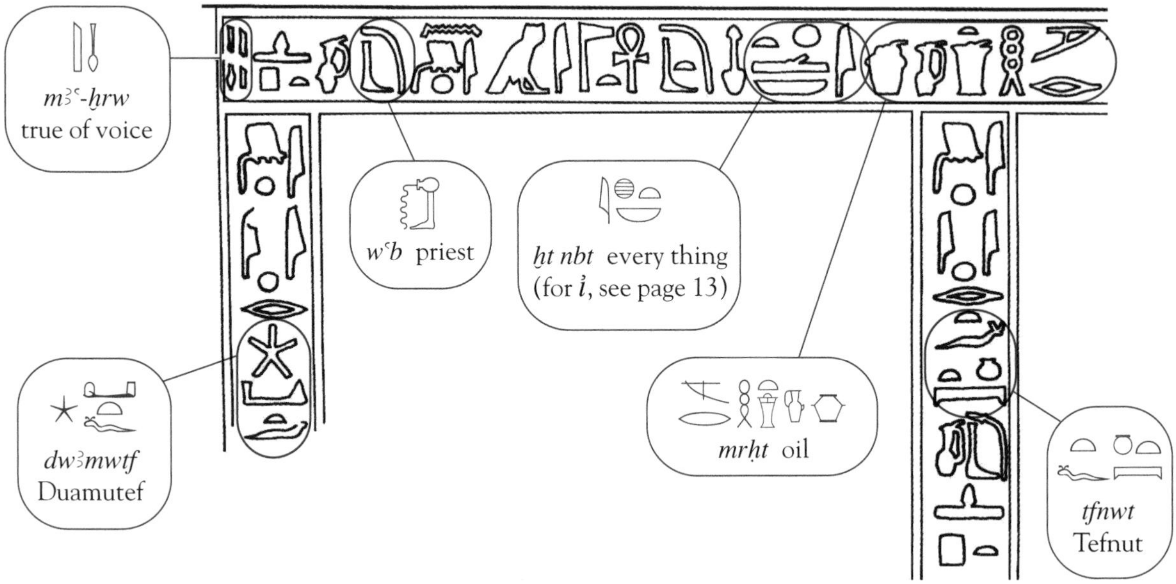

20 The coffin of Khnumhotep with the inscription explained.

inscriptions that have suffered damage. In your wider reading on Ancient Egypt, you may well see inscriptions like Khnumhotep's published as follows:

[ḥtp dỉ nsw ꜣsỉr nb-ḏdw] nṯr ꜥꜣ nb-ꜣbḏw
dỉ.f prt-ḫrw t ḥnḳt kꜣ ꜣpd šs mnḫt ḳbḥw snṯr mrḥt ḫt nbt nfrt wꜥbt ꜥnḫt nṯr ỉm
n ỉmꜣḫw wꜥb ẖnmw-ḥtp

[An offering which the king gives Osiris, lord of Djedu,] great god,
lord of Abydos:
that he may give a voice offering of bread and beer, oxen and fowl,
alabaster and linen, spring water, incense and oil,
every thing perfect and pure which a god lives on,
for the revered one, the priest, Khnumhotep.

In such cases, the square brackets […] indicate where text is now missing from the inscription, so you have restored what you suppose must have been there originally. Now, your confidence with the offering formula is such that it is time to leave them for a while and move on to important hieroglyphic inscriptions of a different kind.

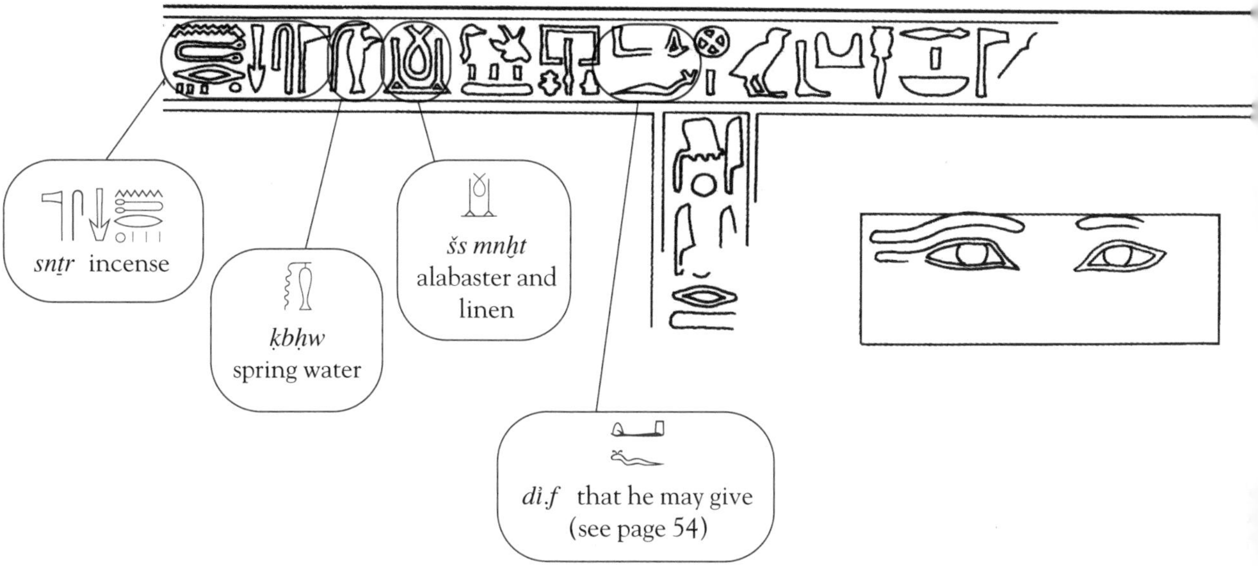

Now practise what you have learned:

– the inscription on the coffin of Khnumhotep, son of Henib

KINGS' NAMES

#23 What You Need to Know: Kings' Titularies

Until this point you have been concentrating on the monuments of high officials because so often they use the offering formula. Now, what is the most typical type of inscription associated with the ancient kings of Egypt? Well, the crucial element of *any* royal inscription is a statement of the identity of the king. This will never simply be a name: it will take the form of his (or, very rarely, her) *titulary*. A titulary is a combination of the different names of the king (most had several names), plus the royal titles and the epithets that associate him with the gods (see **#26**). You can find titularies on the backs of statues, on the bases of the statues, on obelisks, on the walls and gateways of temples, in quarries, on the borders of the realm (such as Sehel Island, see opposite) and even on miniature ceramic scarabs. In fact, titularies decorate the very largest and the smallest of royal monuments. Often nothing else will be written on a royal monument other than the titulary, although on its own it may be long and elaborate. As you will see on page 122, a famous inscription of King Amenhotep III effectively elaborated the king's titulary until it became an important historical statement on its own.

Once again, the good news is that kings' titularies are quite formulaic, so you can learn the typical structure, then get used to the variations that appear on particular monuments. Moreover, although there were dozens and dozens of pharaohs across the centuries, the monuments of certain kings are much more common than those of others, and you will soon get used to seeing a particular

DID YOU KNOW?

You will have noticed that in this book we use the words 'king' and 'pharaoh' interchangeably because this is standard practice in modern times. In fact, using 'pharaoh' as a specific word for one of the kings of Ancient Egypt is something we have adopted from the Bible. The Egyptian phrase 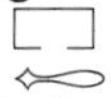 *pr ꜥ3*, which literally means 'great estate', was originally a word for the palace. Only during the New Kingdom did it become a word for the king himself, and only during the 7th century BC did it become a title used with a king's name, such as 'pharaoh Amasis'.

21 Titulary of Senusret III carved in the rocks at Sehel Island.

handful of names. In this part of the book you can learn how to read the principal parts of the titulary, starting with names and titles, and moving on to epithets. The epithets will allow you to explore the nature of the relationship between the king and the gods, and also see how the images of kings and gods interact in monumental art. We can also consider why certain kings' monuments are so much more common than those of others. Once you have worked through this part, you have a list (starting on page 136) of the best-known or more common kings' names, which you can use to check against real monuments.

Stela of Djet, from his Tomb at Abydos (*c.* 2950 BC)

22 Stela of Djet, from Abydos.

The kings of Egypt each had many names. The oldest name – meaning the name used by the earliest kings – is one that identifies him as the sun god, Horus. Horus, you remember, was the son and heir of Osiris (see page 53). Just as Osiris became king in the realm of the dead, so his son became the lawful king in this life. Therefore, each mortal king is the latest incarnation of Horus *ḥrw*, whose name means 'the highest one'. As such, every king in ancient times had a *Horus name*. Typically the Horus name is written inside a device representing the rectangular enclosure and façade of the palace. Above stands the falcon of Horus himself, the creature that flies highest, sees farthest and is swiftest and most ruthless in striking. In this way, the king is stated to be a heavenly presence within the earthly palace. The palace device used to write Horus names was known to the ancients as *srḫ* ('serekh') which means 'that which brings understanding'.

The stela of Djet, now in the Louvre Museum, Paris, was originally one of a pair from his tomb at Abydos, in the cemetery of the first kings (we will see another monument of his later on page 118). His name is written simply as *ḏ*, which most Egyptologists take to be a writing of the word *ḏt* 'cobra'. Some books talk about King 'Cobra', but you are better advised to put the name into English as Djet. On the other hand, the brevity of the writing is a problem. Some Egyptologists read his name instead as an abbreviation of other words or a writing of the name of the snake goddess Wadjyt (see page 27).

This uncertainty in reading royal names is not uncommon, especially among the earliest dynasties, and, together with the lack of vowels in hieroglyphic writing, explains why the name of any king may vary in different history books. Of course, the best way to make sense of such inconsistency in modern books is to do what you are doing now: get to the heart of the problem and learn to read the ancient names yourself.

Stela of Raneb (c. 2750 BC)

23 Stela of Raneb or Nebra, from Saqqara.

The kings of the first three dynasties are usually identified in history books by their Horus names. In fact, the Horus name seems to have been the principal name used by kings until the end of the 3rd millennium BC. A stela of Raneb in the Metropolitan Museum of Art, New York, probably from his tomb at Saqqara, is the only significant monument surviving from his reign, early in the 2nd Dynasty. The name Raneb seems straightforwardly written with ⊙ *rʿ* and 𓎟 *nb*, which together mean 'the Sun is Lord'. However, quite possibly the name employs honorific transposition, in which case the word ⊙ *rʿ* – which is the name of the Sun or, in other words, the sun god – might have been written first, but read last (see page 31). If that were the case, the king's name is Nebra *nbrʿ*, which means something like 'possessor of the qualities of the Sun'. Again uncertainty about exactly how to read the name has created a situation in which some books mention Raneb, while others mention Nebra. There is no way from the writing for you to say which reading is correct.

Inscription of Khakaura Senusret III (c. 1836–1818 BC)

24 Inscription at Sehel with the Horus-name and prenomen of Senusret III.

During the middle of the 3rd millennium BC, the monuments of kings place increasing emphasis on two names normally written inside loops of rope. Today we call these loops *cartouches*, but in ancient texts they are said to represent what the sun goes round; in other words, they are used to state that the named king is king of all the world.

From the 4th Dynasty, one cartouche name became especially important because it was assigned to the king at his accession and remained unique to him. Egyptologists call this name the *prenomen*, although sadly that word does not really tell you anything. Nonetheless, you can usually identify a king's prenomen easily because it is written in a cartouche after the title  *nsw-bỉty*. You already know the word  *nsw*, for example in *ḥtp dỉ nsw* 'an offering which the king gives'. The actual meaning of  *nsw* is as obscure as its reading (see **#12**), although its etymology ('one who belongs to the reeds') may hint at an association with the myth of Horus and the symbolism of palaces and temples. As for  *bỉty* it is another word for 'king', albeit in a different aspect (as the mortal presence in the palace), but its meaning is even more obscure. The combination  *nsw-bỉty* is usually nowadays translated as 'Dual King'. An older translation of  *nsw-bỉty* as 'king of Upper and Lower Egypt', which you will still see used in some Egyptology books, is certainly a misapprehension, based on the erroneous translation into English of a much later Greek version of the title.

From the 5th Dynasty onwards, the prenomen of a king always incorporates Ra  *rʿ*, the name of the Sun. This leads to another simple rule:

- Because of honorific transposition, the sign  is *always* written first *in any prenomen*, but always read last.

For example, the rock inscription opposite shows the prenomen of a king beginning with . However, because of our new rule you can leave  until last. The next sign is  *ḫʿ*, followed by , which reads *kꜣw* (see **#24**). Finally, we can add  *rʿ* to give *ḫʿ-kꜣw-rʿ*, which means something like 'the souls of the Sun are rising'. However, it is a name so you do not have to translate it. Instead, we usually put the name into English as Khakaura. (Some books use Re instead of Ra for  *rʿ*, based on the Coptic word for 'sun' ⲢⲎ (*rē*), in which case you will see the name as Khakaure.)

You can also see from Khakaura's rock inscription that cartouche names did not replace Horus names; instead they sit side by side. The king's Horus name, which is quite distinct from Khakaura, consists of the words  *nṯr* 'god' and  *ḫprw* 'forms' (see **#24**). Presumably it means something like 'a god in forms', but again it is a name, so you do not have to translate it. We usually put it into English as Netjerkhepru or something similar.

#24 What You Need to Know: Writing Plurals

The prenomen of Khakaura includes the word 𓂓𓂓𓂓, which we read *kꜣw* 'souls'. This is the plural of the word 𓂓𓏤 *kꜣ* 'soul' (see **#17**). His Horus name includes the word 𓆣𓅱 *ḫprw* 'forms', which is the plural of a word 𓆣 *ḫpr* 'form'. You can see from the transliterations *kꜣw* and *ḫprw* that, in spoken Egyptian, plural words normally ended with *-w*, just as English plurals often end in *-s* (souls, forms). Sometimes, as with 𓆣𓅱 *ḫprw*, the 𓅱 *-w* ending also appears in writing. However, sometimes the main sign in a word is repeated three times instead to show the plural, as in 𓂓𓂓𓂓 *kꜣw*. (Repeated three times because once is 'singular' and twice is for 'pairs'.) In the case of 𓂓𓂓𓂓 *kꜣw* there is no need to show 𓅱 *-w* at the end because the *idea* of plural has been made quite clear in writing (and, you remember, *-w* is a weak sound often omitted in writing, see page 13). Still, it is best to put *-w* in transliteration to indicate the plural, whether or not it has been written in the hieroglyphs. A third way of writing plurals is to use the determinatives 𓏪 and 𓏥 with or without 𓅱 *-w* (see **#4**). These are alternative ways of writing plurals and they do not create any differences in meaning. So, for example, 𓆣𓅱 and 𓆣𓅱𓏪 and 𓆣𓏪 and 𓆣𓆣𓆣 are four different ways of writing the same word, *ḫprw* 'forms'.

Likewise, the same cartouche name, Khakaura, can be written in different ways, such as (𓇳𓈍𓂓𓂓𓂓) and (𓇳𓈍𓂓𓏪).

DID YOU KNOW?

As you know, one of the virtues of hieroglyphic writing is the flexibility it offered artists for combining words with images. You will meet this flexibility again and again as you read more texts. Often the choice of writing is determined by the space available. For example, repeating signs, as in 𓆣𓆣𓆣, makes the writing of a plural very obvious. However, three strokes side-by-side 𓏥 may fit the plural ending more efficiently alongside another sign, as in the phrase 𓆣𓏥𓆑 *ḫprw.f* 'his forms', while three vertical strokes would fit the plural writing into a smaller space, as 𓆣𓏪.

Another Inscription of Khakaura Senusret III (*c.* 1836–1818 BC)

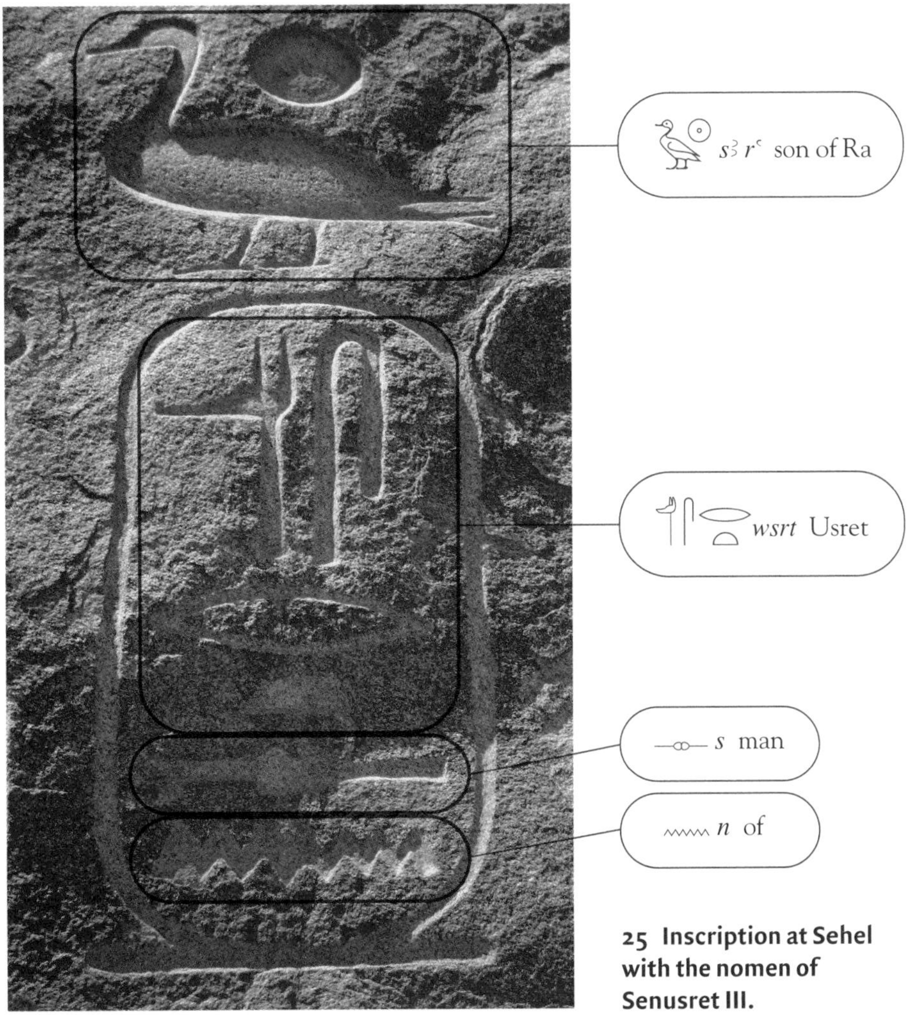

25 Inscription at Sehel with the nomen of Senusret III.

You have now met the Dual King Khakaura, who is also the Horus Netjerkhepru. Yet you will probably not find either of these names in the history books. Why not? Well, both of these names were devised for the king when he came to the throne as the living Horus, whereas our own history books tend to use the name he was given at birth. From the 5th Dynasty onwards, the birth name of the king was usually incorporated into his titulary inside a second cartouche. Today we call this cartouche name the *nomen*, although this term is as meaningless as prenomen. None the less, you can also spot a king's birth name or nomen easily because it is usually written in a cartouche after the title *sꜣ rꜥ* 'son of Ra' or 'son of the Sun'. The implication of this name is that the king is a creature engendered from the same divine substance as the Sun.

The nomen of Khakaura is written with honorific transposition: it starts with the name of the goddess *wsrt* 'Usret', but you read this last. Other than this, you have *s* and *n*, which together mean 'man of', as in Senusret *s-n-wsrt*, 'man of Usret'. (Only the meaning tells us the correct order of the words. Very old Egyptology books talked about the name Usertesen, reading the hieroglyphs in the order they are written, without honorific transposition.) The name Senusret was given to the future king at birth because it was a family name. His father – the king before him – also had the nomen Senusret. In fact, Khakaura was the third of four kings in the same family called Senusret, so the history books usually call him Senusret III (or Senwosret III or something similar). However, the ancients did not use a numbering system for kings who shared the same birth name. Instead, it was the prenomen Khakaura that was unique to this Senusret. So, if you see the name Senusret in an inscription, it could belong to any one of at least four kings, but the prenomen Khakaura tells you which of them exactly.

DID YOU KNOW?

The inscriptions of Senusret III that you have just read are carved directly into a great mass of granite in the river Nile that forms Sehel Island. This is one of many islands at Egypt's traditional border with Nubia, south of Aswan (see page 130). There are dozens of royal inscriptions in this area, on the islands and along the roadsides, and they all exemplify the same basic function. A king's name is a marker, which defines the limits of his activity and the character of the realm his activity has created. The principal responsibility of the pharaoh was to extend his ordered realm into the formless and unpredictable world around. Ancient Egypt viewed the encircling desert in the same light as neighbouring cultures – as a source of potential enrichment with the potential also to overwhelm civilized life. The king had a commitment to uphold Maat *mꜣꜥt*, the principle that there is order in this world, in the face of accident and hostility. Therefore he was believed to be carrying out the will of the Creator in doing so, whether through quarrying stone, building temples, negotiating alliances or going to war.

Now practise what you have learned:

– kings' titularies
– plurals

....

....

....

....

....

....

....

....

....

....

....

....

....

....

....

Three Inscriptions of Ramesses II (c. 1279–1213 BC)

26 Tile inlaid with the prenomen of Ramesses II.

Among the celebrated names of the pharaohs, probably the most famous is Ramesses or  *sꜣ rꜥ rꜥmss* 'the son of Ra, Ramesses'. However, Ramesses was a nomen – a birth name or family name – used by many kings: eleven, in fact, from *c.* 1290 until *c.* 1070 BC. To distinguish the inscriptions of so many Ramesses, we need to know their prenomens. Here we will concentrate on learning the prenomen of Ramesses II, hero of the Battle of Qadesh, and builder of great temples and palaces from Nubia to the Nile

Delta. Undoubtedly there are more surviving inscriptions of Ramesses II than any other individual in Egyptian history, so it is very useful, whether in Egypt or a museum, to be able to recognize his prenomen.

This first example comes from an inlaid tile, now in the British Museum, London. The first thing to note in reading it is that his prenomen is a little (but only a little) more complicated than those you have read so far. Ramesses II is a king of the New Kingdom and, as a general principle, the names of kings were more complicated from the New Kingdom onwards. In this case, as often from this time on, the prenomen is actually in two parts, *each of which has*  *rꜥ written at the start although it is read last because of honorific transposition*. So you can divide his name into  *wsr-mꜣꜥt-rꜥ* 'Usermaatra' and  *stp.n-rꜥ* 'Setepenra'. The first part of Ramesses' name mentions the divine concept of 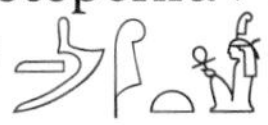 *mꜣꜥt* 'meaningful order' (see page 57), which here is written as though a goddess with the  sign on her head, and means something like, 'the order (*mꜣꜥt*) of the Sun is all-powerful'. The second part means 'one whom the Sun has chosen', based on the word  *stp* 'choose'. Other kings used  *wsr-mꜣꜥt-rꜥ* or  *stp.n-rꜥ* in their prenomens, but the combination of the two together is unique to Ramesses II.

The next example of his prenomen (see figure 27) comes from the base of a colossal statue of the king, one of the pair flanking the main entrance to the Temple of Luxor. Again, you see the same arrangement of signs within the cartouche, even though they are written horizontally, not in a column. However, names of kings were powerful tokens for the ancients, so meaningful elaborations of the hieroglyphs were not uncommon, as you can see here. The image of the goddess  *mꜣꜥt* is now shown holding the sign for  *wsr* 'powerful', as though she were offering it to the king, . Indeed, gods offering symbols to the king is a familiar motif in pharaonic art (see pages 99–105).

Your final example (see figure 28) shows both the prenomen and nomen of Ramesses II as inscribed on a statue of one of his sons, now in The Burrell Collection in Glasgow. First, this inscription uses two titles of the king, which are new to you, but are common, especially from the New Kingdom onwards. Both of these titles are based on the word  *nb* 'lord', a type of title you have already seen, for example, used with Osiris (see **#20**).

The king's prenomen is preceded by the title *nb-tꜣwy* 'lord of the twin lands', in which *t̠ꜣwy* is based on the word *tꜣ* 'land', but written twice to show the idea of a pair (see **#24**). The 'twin lands' are the east and west banks of the Nile and the states of life and afterlife, two distinct ideas brought together through the symbolism of the rising and setting sun. Ramesses' nomen is preceded by the title *nb-ḫꜥw* 'lord of appearances', in which *ḫꜥ* is a word for the spectacular entrance made by the sun at daybreak in Egypt. The king was accustomed to making such appearances himself, clad in brilliant regalia, perhaps on a gilded chariot and often also at daybreak while travelling to a temple (you have seen the word already in the prenomen of Senusret III, page 87). The titles *nb-tꜣwy* and *nb-ḫꜥw* do not replace *nsw-bỉty* and *sꜣ rꜥ*. In fact, the four titles may well be used together in different combinations.

As for Ramesses' names, his prenomen you are now familiar with, but the nomen here seems a little more complicated than . First, the word *rꜥ* 'sun' has been written as though a god with the ⊙ sign on his head. Next, the god *ỉmn* 'Amun' has been included as part of the phrase *mry ỉmn* 'beloved of Amun' (see page 99). In other words, the king's nomen

27 Cartouche of Ramesses II, from the base of a statue in Luxor.

28 Inscription of Ramesses II on a statue of his son, Parahirwenemef.

here reads 'Ramesses, beloved of Amun'. However, the name *ỉmn* has been written beside for the sake of honorific transposition, while the word *mry* 'beloved' has been written in the middle of the cartouche as a sort of pivot for the two parts, 'Ramesses' and 'beloved of Amun'. Finally, to suit the vertical layout of the cartouche, the last *-s* in Ramesses *Rmss* has been written with rather than , but then you already know that these two hieroglyphs are simple alternatives and this choice of sign does not affect the reading in any way (see page 11).

All in all, the cartouche names of Ramesses II are a good, and also extreme, example of how individual hieroglyphs within a cartouche may be written in unusual ways and moved around to create meaningful groups that are not simply part of the name, as when the signs and are combined, or the phrase *mry ỉmn* is broken up to fit the cartouche. Sometimes reading cartouches may seem like one of those children's puzzles in which you have to rearrange tiles until you get the correct picture. As with those puzzles, however, the best guide for your reading is to recognize whose cartouche this is before you begin to analyse the writing. That means becoming familiar with the commonest cartouche names, such as those of Ramesses II – as well as remembering to read the labels in museums. Take heart: if you can cope with the variations in how his prenomen and nomen are written (and presumably, having read this far, you can), then there is nothing for you to fear in the way hieroglyphs are used in the vast majority of other inscriptions. The flexibility used in the layout of kings' cartouche names is as problematic as hieroglyphic writing is liable to become.

DID YOU KNOW?

As we noted on page 51, a major source of confusion for readers of Egyptology books is the way in which the same names of kings may be given in different English versions: Tuthmosis or Thutmose, Ramesses or Ramses. There are two basic practices used by modern authors, each of which has its problems:

- One is to use the forms handed down by classical (Greek and Latin) writers, such as Herodotus and Manetho, which is how we come by Ramesses for 𓇳𓄟𓋴𓋴 *rʿ-ms-s* or 𓇳𓄟𓋴𓇓 *rʿ-ms-sw* (and this is also how we can be sure to read 𓇳 first and not last in this nomen). You can spot most classical forms because they usually end in -es or -is. The main problems here are that classical forms are often not much like the original Egyptian, for example 𓄊𓋴𓂋𓏏𓊃𓈖 *s-n-wsrt* appears in Herodotus' splendid tales as 'Sesostris', while other names, such as Tutankhamun, are not mentioned by classical writers at all.

- Therefore, an increasingly common practice among Egyptologists is to use forms taken directly from the Egyptian. However, the problem here is that no vowels were written in Egyptian, so we cannot be sure how the names were pronounced (see **#3**). According to this way of doing things, we can put the transliteration of 𓄊𓋴𓂋𓏏𓊃𓈖 *s-n-wsrt* into English as 'Senusret'. However, we can be sure that this is not how his name was pronounced. Moreover, Senusret seems rather technical, so some modern authors make the name seem more 'friendly' by devising forms such as 'Senwosret' – taking the 'o' from 'Sesostris'! To add to the confusion, some classical forms, such as 'Ramesses', are so familiar that few people want to abandon them in favour of forms like 'Ramesse' or 'Ramessu', although some writers are keen on the 'friendly' compromise, 'Ramses'.

If this all seems illogical and inconsistent – well, it is. Some authors use Amenophis and Ramesses, some Amenhotep and Ramesses, others prefer Amenhotpe and Ramses. So how can you make sense of this confusion? Once again, the best thing you can do is what you are doing now: learning to read the names in the inscriptions for yourself.

Three Stelae of Thutmose IV (*c.* 1400–1390 BC) from the Great Sphinx

At least 20 stelae were set up by Thutmose IV during a massive operation to hold back the sand that had drifted around the Great Sphinx at Giza. According to a larger stela of the same king, protruding between the paws of the Sphinx to this day (see below), the Sun god appeared in a dream to Thutmose when he was still a prince and promised him the throne in return for clearing away the sand (see **#26**). The modern excavator of the site, Selim Hassan, believed the king built three concentric walls at 10 m (3.3 ft) intervals around the already ancient monument, pushing back the shapeless desert to restore the form of the Sphinx before marking the work with stelae.

29 The Sphinx at Giza, with the top of Thutmose IV's larger stela showing between its forelegs.

#25 What You Need To Know: Epithets

Each of the stelae Thutmose IV erected shows him offering to various gods of the Giza cemetery. The first stela (opposite) embellishes the king's titulary with various epithets or descriptions. Among the commonest epithets applied to Egyptian kings is *dỉ ꜥnḫ*, 'given life', or the fuller variation *dỉ ꜥnḫ ḏd wꜣs*, 'given life, stability and authority'. As often as not this epithet is written after one of the cartouche names of the king; in the case of this stela, Thutmose's prenomen *mn-ḫprw-rꜥ*, written with (see **#24**). Either version of the epithet may be qualified by the phrase *mỉ rꜥ* 'like the Sun' (written with honorific transposition). So, here and at ❶ in figure 31 you can see: *mn-ḫprw-rꜥ dỉ ꜥnḫ mỉ rꜥ* 'Menkheprura, given life like the Sun'.

The implication is that the king, like the Sun, will be reborn every day until the end of time, which is consistent with the symbolism of the titles *nb-tꜣwy* 'lord of the twin lands' and *nb-ḫꜥw* 'lord of appearances', which you met on pages 93–94.

With practice, you will come to expect epithets based on *dỉ ꜥnḫ* whenever you come across a cartouche, so your reading here will come to be guided by your expectations. However, notice also how the phrase runs from left to right across the stela (as indicated by arrow 1 below), so is orientated with the king, whereas the signs in front of the goddess read the opposite way.

DID YOU KNOW?

As you read the inscriptions of Thutmose IV you will begin to see how the titulary of the king elaborates upon his titles and names by adding epithets that talk about his authority and his relationship with the gods. Epithets are standard descriptive tags, which can sometimes become associated with individuals, such as 'Richard the Lionheart' or 'The King of Rock'n'Roll'. However, we tend to use epithets in a standard way to associate somebody's name with a particular status or authority, such as 'His Holiness, Pope Benedict', 'Her Majesty, the Queen' or, indeed, 'Mr President'. Likewise, the epithets used of kings in Egyptian inscriptions are quite standard, so they appear often and are well worth learning.

30 Stela of Thutmose IV offering to Isis, lady of the sky, from Giza.

Another extremely common epithet is based on the word *mry* 'beloved', which describes the king as 'beloved of [god so-and-so]'. The epithet can be written in various ways based on the alternative signs 𓌸 or 𓈘 (see page 94). The final 𓇌 *-y* may or may not be shown, so possible writings include 𓌸 or 𓌸𓇌 and 𓈘 or 𓈘𓇌. As you may expect by now, the writing of this epithet will use honorific transposition, so you have another simple rule:

- Epithets based on 𓌸𓇌 *mry* 'beloved' translate 'king X beloved of god Y', but the name *and titles* of the god will be written in front of *mry*. By the way, in epithets, as in titles you will not usually find a separate word for 'of' (see page 23).

31 Stela of Thutmose IV from Giza (figure 30), with the directions of the text marked.
❶ Menkheprura, given life like the Sun /
❷ beloved of /
❸ Isis, lady of the sky

In Thutmose's stela you see the sign (marked with a 2) following the name of the goddess *ꜣst* 'Isis', who is said to be *nbt-pt* 'lady of the sky'. (The title *nbt* is the female counterpart of *nb* 'lord', see **#18** and page 23). However, you read *mry ꜣst nbt-pt* 'beloved of Isis, lady of the sky' because you always transliterate and translate *mry* in the place where it makes sense – between the king's name and god's name – and not where it is written. Who is beloved of Isis? Of course, it is the king, so we can read the whole stela as a single inscription:

❶ *mn-ḫprw-rꜥ dỉ ꜥnḫ mỉ rꜥ* ❷ *mry* ❸ *ꜣst nbt-pt*

❶ Menkheprura, given life like the Sun / ❷ beloved of /
❸ Isis, lady of the sky.

The different parts of the inscription have been written so as to be orientated with the figures (king or goddess) to which they refer, but the sense of the whole thing dictates that you read them together. Likewise, the actual figures of the king and the goddess are separate, but clearly interact in the scene.

Now you can apply exactly the same pattern to two more of Thutmose's stelae. The next one for you to read (figure 32, overleaf) gives the king's prenomen and nomen (more on this below) followed by the epithet  *dỉ ꜥnḫ*. His names are preceded by another title new to you, but actually very common and well worth copying out to learn. The title is  *nṯr nfr* 'perfect god', which seems odd to modern minds because it implies another divinity who is less than perfect. However, the king is  *nṯr nfr* 'perfect god' because – like us but unlike the gods and the dead – he is part of this mortal life, whereas – unlike us but like the gods and the justified dead – he is in the state of adoration (see **#19**). This is why he may act as the intermediary between the two states. (It may interest you that the Egyptian word  *nfr* 'perfect' is analogous to 'zero', a concept which sits between the opposed states of positive and negative, but remains distinct from either.)

Now, seeing the king in the presence of another figure, you may switch on your radar to scan for the word *mry* 'beloved' and sure enough you will find  written above the head of the female figure. So, you can assume that she is a goddess, and that the remaining hieroglyphs above her write her name and title. In fact, she is  *sšꜣt* 'Seshat', described as  *nbt-sẖ* 'lady of writing'.

As for the king's names, his prenomen you already know (see page 98), but his nomen needs some explanation. Like Ramesses II, Thutmose IV belongs to the New Kingdom and his names may be written in quite complex ways. For example, his birth name, Thutmose, is written simply enough as  *ḏḥwty-ms* including the name of the god  *ḏḥwty* 'Thoth', which is the 'Thut' part of 'Thutmose'. In this case *ḏḥwty* is read first, not with honorific transposition: 'Thoth is born'. However, within the cartouche of his nomen, an epithet  *ḫꜥ ḫꜥw* has been added to his birth name and the signs have been moved about to fill the available space in 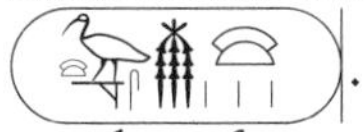. The epithet  *ḫꜥ ḫꜥw* means something like 'most spectacular of appearances' (see page 94).

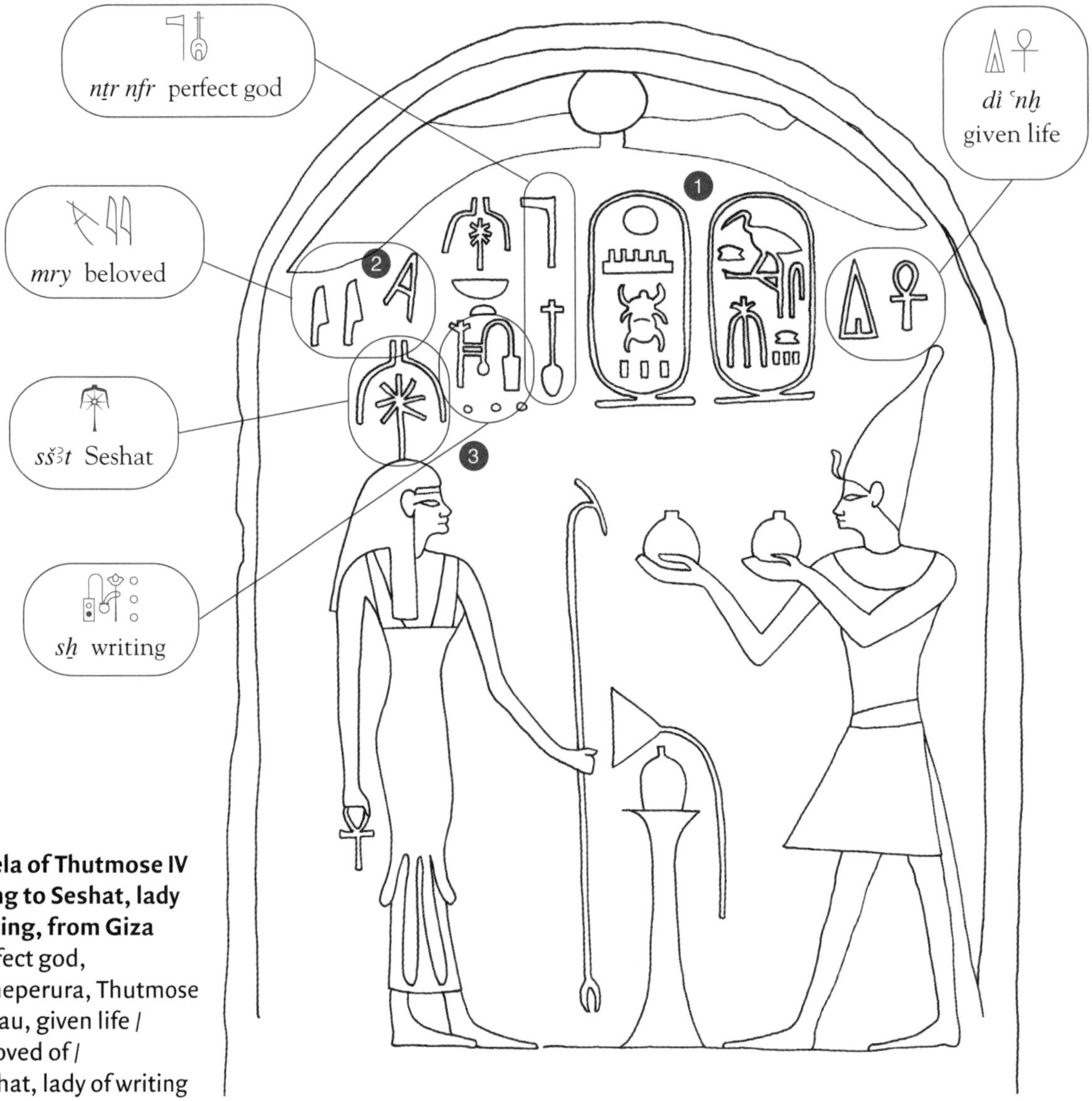

32 Stela of Thutmose IV offering to Seshat, lady of writing, from Giza
❶ Perfect god, Menkheperura, Thutmose Khakhau, given life /
❷ beloved of /
❸ Seshat, lady of writing

So hopefully you now have a transliteration and translation something like:

❶ *nṯr nfr mn-ḫprw-rꜥ ḏḥwty-ms ḫꜥ-ḫꜥw dỉ ꜥnḫ* ❷ *mry* ❸ *sšꜣt nbt-sẖ*

❶ Perfect god, Menkheprura, Thutmose Khakhau, given life /
❷ beloved of / ❸ Seshat, lady of writing.

The same thought process will allow you to read the top part of the final stela from around the Great Sphinx (we will return to the inscription in the coloured box in **#26** below). The only unpredictable element is the identity

33 Stela of Thutmose IV offering to Hathor, lady of sycamore, from Giza.
❶ Perfect god, Menkheperura, given life / ❷ beloved of / ❸ Hathor, lady of sycamore

of the goddess, who is *ḥwt-ḥr* 'Hathor', titled *nbt-nht* 'lady of sycamore'. Knowing her identity, you can arrive at a transliteration and translation something like the following:

❶ *nṯr nfr mnḫprwrꜥ dỉ ꜥnḫ* ❷ *mry* ❸ *ḥwt-ḥr nbt-nht*

❶ Perfect god, Menkheprura, given life / ❷ beloved of / ❸ Hathor, lady of sycamore.

#26 The King and the Gods

The scenes in the stelae of Thutmose IV are framed by what Egyptologists call a lunette: a rounded top representing the arc of the sky surmounted by the sun disc in its zenith. Wings on the sun disc indicate that it is moving – tracing its course from sunrise to sunset. This course defines both the pattern of life and the extent of the king's domain, symbolized also by his cartouches (see page 86).

Between the earth underfoot and the sky above, the critical activity of this earth is presented as the interaction between the king and the gods. Their relationship is shown on a human scale and predicated on mutual 'love'; it is intimate and equal, and king and god are shown acting each for the benefit of the other. Typically the king makes offerings, while the gods reciprocate by handing him the sceptre of *wꜣs* 'authority' and the hieroglyph *ꜥnḫ* 'life' (and look also at page 118). In other words, the king receives the right to govern in this life from the divine realm, and conducts his own affairs as a means of adoring the gods.

What does the king offer and why? On page 100 he offers what look like long, bell-flowered stalks of lotus. On pages 102 and 103 he offers jars, presumably of some liquid or unguent, but how can you tell? In fact, the inscription within the coloured box on page 103 tells you exactly what is happening. *It is a caption.* You have already met a caption involving the phrase *dbḥt ḥtp* 'asked-for offerings' on page 65, but here the caption involves an action, *rdỉt* 'giving'. The word *rdỉt* is a special form of the word or *rdỉ* 'give' that is suited to captions, just as in English we often caption photographs using words with *-ing* ('The Queen *leaving* Buckingham Palace yesterday with crowds *looking* on'). However, for present purposes you do not need to worry about the grammar, just make use of 'giving' as the most typical strategy for writing captions in English. What is the king 'giving'? He is giving *ḳbḥw* 'water' (more specifically, artesian or spring water), so you read *rdỉt ḳbḥw* 'giving water'.

Why does he do this? Well, the Egyptian statement tells us he offers water *ỉr.f dỉ ꜥnḫ* 'so he may carry out the given life'. As with the word *rdỉt* 'giving', likewise *ỉr.f* 'so he may carry out' is a special form of the word *ỉrỉ* 'do' or 'carry out' (specifically, it is a form that allows you to talk about *the future*). Again, you do not have to worry about the grammar because  *ir.f di ꜥnḫ* is a standard phrase, which you can simply memorize, then look for it wherever you find a scene of the king offering to the gods. The phrase is not uncommon, especially in temples from the New Kingdom onwards, although, of course, in another inscription the king may well offer something else instead of  *ḳbḥw* 'water'. An interesting point to note is that the hieroglyphs at the beginning of this phrase  *rdit ḳbḥw* are always orientated with the king, whereas those at the end  *ir.f di ꜥnḫ* are usually orientated with the god (although '*he*' must be the king, of course, because it cannot be the goddess).

Anyhow, you can read 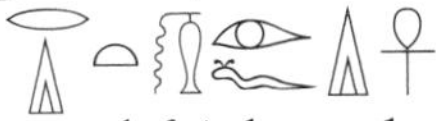 *rdit ḳbḥw ir.f di ꜥnḫ* 'giving water so he may carry out the given life', but what does it mean? Its meaning is not obvious because here you are delving deep into ancient Egyptian religious thought. You already know about the concept of  *di ꜥnḫ* 'given life' in relation to the king (see page 98), and now you are being told that the king offers to the gods because that is the conduct required from him to fulfil the  *ꜥnḫ* 'life' he has been given.

At least, that is one explanation, although other scholars may well dispute this. What matters here is that you are finding your own feet and making sense of the ancient sources rather than relying on the interpretations of others. So, there you have it: the scenes on Thutmose's stelae, erected at one of the most ancient religious sites in Egypt, show you the interaction between the king and the gods, while the inscriptions tell you that the relationship is founded on the recognizably human principles of love and respect.

DID YOU KNOW?

Stelae mark out ground where the king and other gods meet, although, like Thutmose's dream (see page 97), 'meetings' were not necessarily arranged by the king. The king is shown as the principal in almost every scene of worship. During ceremonies, he was present in the actions of the priest, a belief embodied in the priestly title  *ḥm-nṯr* 'god's body' (see page 31). On its own *ḥm* is the standard word for the king's presence.

Now practise what you have learned:

– the titularies of Ramesses II and Thutmose IV
– epithets

....

....

....

....

....

....

....

....

....

....

....

....

....

....

....

Inscriptions from a Golden Shrine of Tutankhamun (c. 1332–1322 BC)

The discovery in 1922 of the tomb of Tutankhamun was the defining moment of modern Egyptology. The unprecedented confluence of antiquity, modern media coverage and unsuspected treasure unleashed the torrent of books, movies and documentaries that dominates popular Egyptology to this day. Tutankhamun reigned during the New Kingdom, when Egypt was the richest

34 Golden shrine of Tutankhamun housing his internal organs, from his tomb in Thebes.

and most influential nation on earth. Though other Egyptian royal tombs have been discovered nearly intact, none is from this era. Egypt's location at the junction of Africa, Asia and Europe made the land a focus for every kind of exchange – whether in commodities, diplomats, or ideas – and she could utilize her enormous wealth founded on the gold mines of Nubia (see page 50). A contemporary king of Assyria remarked that 'gold is in Egypt like the sands of the desert', and the innermost of Tutankhamun's three coffins was crafted out of 100 kg (220 lb) of gold.

None the less, even in this most singular of archaeological sites, what you have learned so far holds true. Here we will look at just three of the hundreds of inscriptions within the burial of Tutankhamun, but they are sufficient to illustrate how much more accessible this famous discovery has become for you now you can read hieroglyphs. The inscriptions are on a gilded wooden shrine erected around a stone chest, which in turn held four miniature gold coffins containing the king's mummified internal organs. In other words, these inscriptions were placed in immediate proximity to the king's body parts to label whose remains they are. The first inscription (right) is on the canopy of the shrine and contains a cartouche name with two titles you know. One is *nsw* 'king', the other is *nb-tꜣwy* 'lord of the twin lands'. After the cartouche is another phrase you know, *mꜣꜥ-ḫrw* 'true of voice' (see page 57).

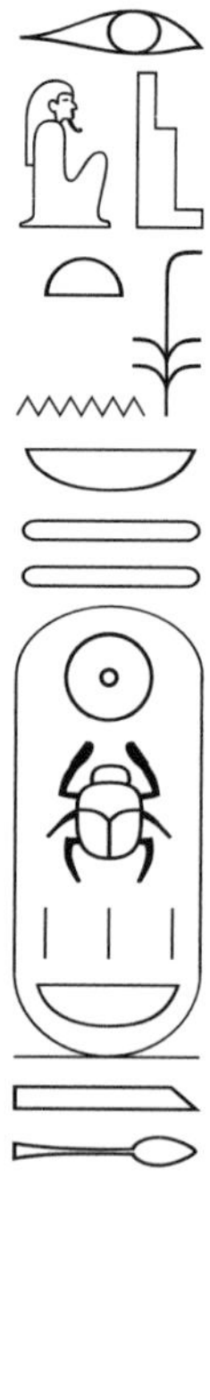

At the beginning of the inscription is the name *ꜣsỉr* 'Osiris'. So straight away you can read *ꜣsỉr nsw nb-tꜣwy* [cartouche-name] *mꜣꜥ-ḫrw* 'Osiris, king, lord of the twin lands [name], true of voice'. In fact, the king's name is the only element in this inscription that you do not already know. This is his prenomen, which is usually written , but here written with *nb* at the end because it neatly fills the bottom of a vertical cartouche. On the basis of the usual writing you can read *nb-ḫprw-rꜥ* 'Nebkheprura', which is comparable to *mn-ḫprw-rꜥ*, the prenomen of his great-grandfather, Thutmose IV (see page 98). Thinking back to the remarks about Osiris earlier in the book, notice how the dead king is identified with Osiris by using the god's name as part of his title. This became standard practice when naming dead people from the

New Kingdom onwards (almost like writing, 'the *late* king, lord of the twin lands, etc.'). However, the identification seems especially poignant and profound in an inscription that labels the dismembered remains of a king, because that was the original fate of Osiris (see page 53).

The second inscription (right) also comes from the canopy of the shrine, and includes the king's nomen, which you already know must read something like 'Tutankhamun'. Anyway, look at the inscription and you can recognize the name *ꜣsỉr* 'Osiris' plus the title that usually precedes a nomen, which is *sꜣ rꜥ* 'son of Ra'. Again, after the cartouche, is the epithet *mꜣꜥ-ḫrw* 'true of voice', so you have the same pattern as in the previous inscription: *ꜣsỉr sꜣ rꜥ* [cartouche name] *mꜣꜥ-ḫrw* 'Osiris, son of Ra [name], true of voice'. However, the phrase *mꜣꜥ-ḫrw* has been extended with the word *ḫr* 'before' to create *mꜣꜥ-ḫrw ḫr ỉt.f* 'true of voice before his father' (see page 26).

So you are only left with the king's nomen. Like other New Kingdom names you have seen, this is slightly complicated because it includes an epithet within the cartouche, written in a very abbreviated manner as *ḥḳꜣ ỉwnw šmꜥ* 'ruler of Heliopolis of Upper Egypt'. *ỉwnw* 'Heliopolis' was the community sacred to Ra, the Sun (*ỉwnw* is transcribed as 'On' in the Bible). However, *ỉwnw šmꜥ* 'Heliopolis of Upper Egypt' is a reference to Thebes, where the tomb of Tutankhamun lies in the Valley of the Kings. Leaving those three signs aside, the cartouche begins with the name of a god, *ỉmn* 'Amun', so you can anticipate that there may be honorific transposition. Then you have three simple sounds *twt* followed by a familiar sign *ꜥnḫ*. Obviously together these are the sounds of *twt-ꜥnḫ-ỉmn* 'Tutankhamun'. So, there is honorific transposition, although you would not know just from the writing whether to read Amun at the beginning or end of the king's name. In fact, we only know the correct reading from the meaning of the name, which is 'the living image (*twt*) of Amun'. So this is another instance where you simply have to follow established practice in reading the king's name.

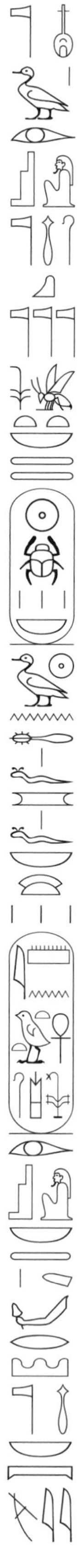

The third inscription (right), running down one of the posts of the shrine, gives a fuller writing of the king's titulary, including both his prenomen and his nomen, as you would expect from the presence of two cartouches. The first cartouche is his prenomen *nb-ḫprw-rꜥ*, so what titles do you recognize in front of it? Hopefully *nṯr nfr* 'perfect god' and *nsw-bỉty* 'Dual King' and *nb-tꜣwy* 'lord of the twin lands'. What else is there, between *nṯr nfr* and *nsw-bỉty*? Well, hopefully you can also recognize the word *sꜣ* 'son' and the name of Osiris *ꜣsỉr*, so put them together and you have *sꜣ ꜣsỉr* 'son of Osiris'. When you get the name of a god, you often get one or more of the god's titles as well. Sure enough, here you get two: Osiris is said to be *nṯr ꜥꜣ* 'great god' (see **#20**) and also *ḥḳꜣ nṯrw* 'ruler of the gods'.

Notice how Osiris' titles, while distinct, are comparable to those of the king: both are gods *nṯr nfr* versus *nṯr ꜥꜣ*; and both are rulers *ḥḳꜣ ỉwnw šmꜥ* versus *ḥḳꜣ nṯrw*.

The second cartouche in this inscription is the king's nomen *twt-ꜥnḫ-ỉmn*, so what titles do you recognize in front of it? Hopefully you will find *sꜣ rꜥ* 'son of Ra' and *nb-ḫꜥw* 'lord of appearances'. The title *sꜣ rꜥ* is extended in a typical way with the phrase *n ẖt.f* 'of his belly', which emphasizes the common substance of the king and the Sun (see pages 84 and 90). Then there is an epithet based on the word *mry* 'beloved' (see page 99). In this case, the phrase *mry.f* means 'his beloved'. Notice how both *n ẖt.f* and *mry.f* use the word *.f* 'he' or 'his' (see **#15**).

Now, because this is a king's titulary perhaps you immediately scanned all the way through to see what you recognize. If you do, you will see that the hieroglyphs following the king's name depend upon the word *mry* 'beloved'. This then reminds you of the rule on page 99 that you read 'king X *beloved of* god Y' even though the name and titles of the god will be written in front of *mry*. Who is the god? He is *ꜣsỉr* Osiris, described as *nṯr ꜥꜣ* 'great god' and *nb-pt* 'lord of the sky' (see page 67). Here he also has another title which is typical of him,  *nb-tꜣ ḏsr* 'lord of the sacred land', in which  *tꜣ ḏsr* 'the sacred land' refers to the ritual areas of Abydos.

Now, put all these elements together and the inscription tells you:

> *nṯr nfr sꜣ ꜣsỉr nṯr ꜥꜣ ḥḳꜣ nṯrw nsw-bỉty nb-tꜣwy nb-ḫprw-rꜥ*
> *sꜣ rꜥ n ẖt.f mry.f nb-ḫꜥw twt-ꜥnḫ-ỉmn ḥḳꜣ ỉwnw šmꜥ*
> *mry ꜣsỉr nb-tꜣ ḏsr nṯr ꜥꜣ nb-pt*
> Perfect god, son of Osiris, the great god and ruler of the gods, lord of the twin lands, Nebkheprura; son of Ra of his belly, his beloved, lord of appearances, Tutankhamun, ruler of Heliopolis of Upper Egypt; beloved of Osiris, lord of the sacred land, great god, lord of the sky.

Perhaps now you understand a little better how much faith and commitment the Ancient Egyptians invested in the burial of any king, who was the real and present incarnation of Osiris – the first mortal and the first to pass from this life into the state of adoration beyond. After all is said and done, it turns out that Tutankhamun's golden burial is not a statement about wealth and power, but about the divinity and eminence of a pharaoh.

THE OLDEST TEXTS AND EARLIEST HIEROGLYPHS

#27 How Did Writing Begin in Egypt?

If hieroglyphs are not picture writing, why would people use pictures to write? The obvious answer is that they can both be beautiful and add information to beautiful art. Presumably you are reading this book now because hieroglyphs have caught your eye, possibly more than any other form of writing. In fact, to write letters, accounts, reports, stories and suchlike, the few ancient Egyptians who were literate wrote, with ink and a brush, in a script we now call *hieratic*.

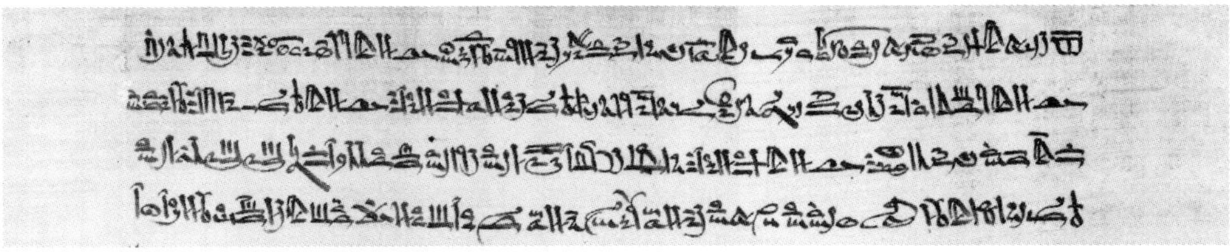

35 Part of the Great Harris papyrus from Thebes, around 1155 BC, showing a hieratic text.

The two forms of writing are rarely used together, so hieratic need not concern us in this book.The writing principles of hieratic are the same as for hieroglyphs, but the forms are cursive and often joined up, like our own handwriting. The much more elaborate hieroglyphs, used only in sacred contexts, were carved or painted or inlaid, frequently using materials such as ivory or gold. Moreover, hieroglyphs were a gift from the king and the earliest inscriptions – dating to 3000 BC or perhaps a little earlier – were devised for monuments to the gods or for use in royal burials (see pages 114 to 121).

None the less, perhaps you will object that, at the beginning of history, mankind was more primitive, so writing must have been picture writing back then and only became more sophisticated through time (see **#13**). At present, there is no unambiguous evidence to support this assumption. For one, there is no apparent period of 'primitive' writing in Egypt, when pictures were used to write crude statements or accounts, such as we find in the earliest texts from

Mesopotamia. Moreover, taking into account the vagaries of what is liable to survive in the archaeological record, the use of hieratic writing on perishable materials such as papyrus or leather seems to be as old in Egypt as hieroglyphic writing on monuments. Hieroglyphs were certainly developed and refined in the early centuries of the 3rd millennium BC, but this was a process ongoing until Roman times. The earliest surviving inscriptions use basically the same writing principles as those you have already learned in order to write the sounds of Egyptian.

Hieroglyphs developed by means of the rebus principle. Rebus is writing that adapts pictures to write sounds, in the same way that we could write the English word 'believes' as  'bee-leaves'. The word 'believes' has nothing to do with 'bees' or 'leaves', the last two words just happen to sound the same as the sounds that make up the word 'believes'. We could write whole English phrases in this way, such as  'Eye Bee-Leaf Ewe' and  'Eye Bee-Leaf Hair'. It would be meaningless to try to make sense of these pictures, but the corresponding sounds in English do make sense (although these particular examples would be gibberish in Egyptian or another language). Still, a rebus is a clumsy way of writing unless we all agree on which signs to use and how to read them, which in turn suggests that hieroglyphic writing in Egypt was a deliberate invention – presumably at the palace? – rather than an accidental discovery. So, let us look at some of the earliest inscriptions that have survived from Egypt, using an array of objects dating to the reigns of three of the first four kings.

DID YOU KNOW?

Even in the ancient world, the Egyptians had a reputation as impressive record keepers with detailed accounts of their earliest kings. In Egyptian terms this means their accounts reach back to the moment the Earth was created, so their own king-lists do not make the distinction we do between myths and history. For example, as you know, Osiris was believed to be very real and his tomb could be visited at Abydos. On the other hand, several king-lists from the 2nd and 1st millennia mention a king called Menes, who is said to have founded the great Egyptian metropolis of Memphis, which may in turn mark the beginning of history as we understand it. However, the historical identity, or even the existence, of Menes is much disputed by scholars today. As a result, the first king of Egypt for whom we have undoubted historical records is Narmer, whom you will meet in the next section.

Slate Palette of King Narmer from the Temple of Horus (*c.* 2950 BC)

36 The palette of Narmer from Hieraconpolis.

The palette of King Narmer is from a splendid early temple at Hieraconpolis dedicated to Horus, the god most associated with kingship in later eras. Narmer was the first historical king of Egypt, and his exquisite slate monument has become an icon of the dawn of human history, although its original function is unclear. It is called a palette because its shape is based on smaller objects used for grinding cosmetics, but this is an altogether larger (63 cm, 24.8 in. high) and more impressive monument. As noted above, the earliest kings and earliest inscriptions seem to go hand in hand, and here you can see signs which are undoubtedly hieroglyphic writing. In other words they can be understood using the same principles used for hieroglyphic writing in later royal monuments, such as those you read in the previous sections.

For example, next to the king is a standing figure at ❶ opposite, holding a pair of sandals and there are two signs beside him, which are perfectly legible as hieroglyphs, although not as pictures. The 2-sound sign *ḥm* is used in all eras of Ancient Egypt to write the word *ḥm* 'servant', while is used in early monuments to write words associated with 'king'. The actual reading of is a problem: some scholars read it as *ḥrw* 'Horus', others as *wr* 'chief'. However, its basic meaning is widely accepted, so you may put the words together (assuming honorific transposition) to read *ḥm ḥrw* 'servant of Horus' or *ḥm wr* 'servant of the chief', or suchlike. This seems an appropriate identity for a character following the king and carrying his sandals.

is a sign that dropped out of use after the earliest centuries of writing, just as in English we no longer use the letters ð and þ, although we still use the sounds they write. On the other hand, *ḥm* was retained in use, and another feature familiar from later texts is the palace-façade sign used for writing the name of the king at ❷. This is the device used to enclose the Horus name of every king (see page 84). Within it you see two hieroglyphs known from later periods to read *nʿr* and *mr*, so you may take *nʿrmr* 'Narmer' to be the king's name.

Because the king's name is marked as such, you know what is going on. However, the hieroglyphs at ❸ and ❹ are more of a problem. They seem to label figures, but what do they say? Are they also names? According to their use in later texts the signs at ❸ read *wʿ š*, which may mean something like 'leader (*wʿ*) of Lake-land (*š*)', or may instead be a name *wʿš*

37 The palette of Narmer from Hieraconpolis with positions of text marked.

'Wash'. If it is a name, is it that of the man, his tribe, his nation? The problem here is that early inscriptions generally lack the determinatives (see **#4**) and sound complements (see **#7**) that clarify matters in later texts.

Likewise, the signs at ❹ are well known in later texts. 𓊅 is usually a determinative for words to do with 'build' or 'wall' and 𓎺 writes either *sꜣ* 'protection' or 'tent', but what do they mean here? Perhaps all walled and tented communities have been laid low? Perhaps a town called *sꜣ* 'Sa' has been laid low? We can speculate – but how can we know? This ambiguity is typical of the earliest inscriptions.

However, underpinning this ambiguity is the crux of the point raised in this part of the book: why did the ancients use pictures to write? It is, indeed, a matter of beauty and art, but also about recognizing that words and images are not entirely separate. Look to ❺ now, and you see an obvious but cryptic symbol. A symbol of what? From your understanding of inscriptions so far, perhaps you will suppose that the human-armed falcon is Horus or the king? The captive he is leading by the nose is either a man or the representative of a community: perhaps a man from the marshes indicated by the reeds, or from a lake land according to the pool shape of his body? Then, you may also remember that the 'reed' 𓆼 as a hieroglyph reads *ḫꜣ* 'thousand' (see page 64–65), and here you see six of them. So, is Horus presenting Narmer with a man or a community from the lakes? Or more specifically with 6,000 captives? Where do the pictures end and the words begin?

DID YOU KNOW?

The fact that a royal monument is made of stone may seem obvious, but it is not insignificant. As you know, the Ancient Egyptians inscribed hieroglyphs in stone to create powerful art; art that lets you comprehend the presence of a god-king. Now, we may be tempted to view such scenes as a sort of photographic record of early historical events, but religious art is not a simple record of the world. It can say things more profound. So, Narmer is shown crushing his enemies with a club, but what does this really mean in the heart of the temple? Certainly, the king clubbing his enemies remained a dominant image in temple decoration until the days of the last pharaohs. For most Egyptians it would have been such scenes, often towering over their communities, that were familiar, not glimpses of pharaoh in person. A poem from the 13th century BC describes the king as he appears at war, and does so by using word associations ('As for the spokes (*ꜥsr* in Egyptian) of your chariot: the fearful (*ꜥrs*) of every land'). In effect, the poet must have been standing outside a temple thinking how to make sense of the scene of the king at war, detail by detail ('this means such, and this means such, etc.'). The crucial point is that the poet did not see a broadcast or memorial of the king's particular victories. What he saw was the king's unbridled authority over the world in its length and breadth (see page 127).

Ivory Comb of King Djet from his Tomb (c. 2950 BC)

Despite the difficulties of an artefact as complex as Narmer's palette, the basic principles of hieroglyphic writing are demonstrably present, so not everything in early texts need be speculative. For example, on this simple treasure not only hieroglyphs, but also beliefs mentioned in later inscriptions, are unequivocally apparent. As this is an ivory comb for the locks of King Djet, the ruler's Horus name is clearly written within the palace device (see page 84). Above his name a pair of wings transport the falcon Horus in a boat through the sky. To either side, the scene is framed by a pair of sceptres, which not only raise up the sky, but also write 𓌀 *wꜣs* 'authority'. Within this frame is an early version of the sign 𓋹, which writes *ꜥnḫ* 'life'. Taken as a whole the composition of words and images seems to suggest that the world defined by the path of the moving sun is also the full extent of the authority of the king, who is given life. This is an early statement – from the tomb of only the third historical king – of a belief attested in every subsequent era of Egyptian history (see **#26**).

38 Ivory comb of Djet, from his tomb at Abydos.

Ivory Label of King Den from his Tomb
(c. 2900 BC)

39 Ivory label of Den with the phrase 'first occasion of slaughtering the east', from his tomb at Abydos.

The last of these most ancient texts for you to read is a label (as shown by the perforation in the top right for tying). It is a decorated ivory label: for a pair of sandals. Are sandals really so valuable? Well, this label takes the iconic image of the king from Narmer's slate palette, and gives it a special twist. Do you see what this is? Remember what the servant accompanying Narmer was doing: carrying his sandals. The picture here makes graphically clear that a king treads on enemies, so sandals are weapons of war and symbols of power. Notice also that Narmer apparently treads enemies among formless lakes, while Den does his treading upon the formless desert: so sandals are also instruments able to impress form (see page 90). No wonder they are so valuable among the burials of pharaohs.

The hieroglyphs at ❶ (overleaf) presumably catch your eye first; these, as you know, are his Horus name, and 𓂧𓈖 *dn* 'Den' means 'Crusher' in Egyptian.

Some scholars do suggest more cryptic readings, such as 'Giver of water', but there is no compelling need to adopt such explanations, which push at the limits of what you have learned so far.

The scene is framed by inscriptions at ❷ and ❸. At ❷ you see four well-known hieroglyphs, which read *sp tpy* 'first occasion', then for *sḳ* 'slaughter' and for *ỉꜣbt* 'east'. Evidently they write a caption, so remember your translation strategy for actions (here *sḳ* 'slaughter') in captions, which is to use the *-ing* form in English (**#26**). So read the words together as the caption *sp tpy sḳ ỉꜣbt* 'first occasion of slaughtering the east' (remember, in Egyptian, there is often no word that prompts you to use English 'of').

The hieroglyphs at ❸ are also well known, but what they say here is another problem. Perhaps the simplest solution is to read two words writing *ỉn* 'it is' (see **#21**) and writing *kꜣ* 'bull/ox', which you know from the offering formula (see **#10**). The two words are graphically intertwined for spacing reasons (see **#8**), but the reading would simply be *ỉn kꜣ* 'it is the bull'. Who is the bull? The king, of course. This is an equation known in monuments of all periods, and shown here – as in every other image of the king you see in this book – by the fact that he wears a bull's tail at his back.

40 Ivory label of Den, with the inscription explained.

Other readings are possible because there is ambiguity in these early texts. None the less, the hieroglyphic inscription at ❷ suggests that you need to understand ❸ in terms of Egyptian words rather than by looking at the signs as pictures.

What about the inscription beside the fallen enemy at ❹? Not surprisingly, perhaps, it is as cryptic as the inscription beside the stricken enemy in Narmer's palette. Does it belong with the enemy or with the king? Is it a statement or a name? The signs themselves seem recognizable as hieroglyphs, but that in itself does not make the reading clear. Of course,  *n* you know, while ∩ is a sign most often used as the numeral '10' (Egyptian *mḏw*). The sign  is the most difficult: could it be an early version of  a determinative for 'land', or  a determinative for 'district', or even the 2-sound sign 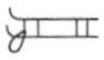 *tm*? However you identify the signs, they could be read as various more or less likely phrases, such '10 districts'; '10 men from canal places'; or '10 eliminated by (me)'. On the other hand, they may simply write an obscure name.

Taken together, these 5,000-year-old monuments demonstrate the basics of the earliest hieroglyphic inscriptions. Yes, many are cryptic, but most are not. Moreover, when you can read these inscriptions you see that the writing principles apply much as they will until the very last hieroglyphic inscriptions. Crucially, when read this way they record themes about the king and gods that you see later in history. Indeed, the powerful new image you have encountered here, the king treading a world of enemies, will become a principal feature of Egyptian monumental art until the coming of Christianity closed the last temples – at a time nearer to you, the reader, than to Narmer, the first king.

PUTTING IT ALL TOGETHER: TWO INSCRIPTIONS

You have acquired impressive skills. Some involve hieroglyphs themselves – how to read signs and recognize words. Some involve your knowledge of Egyptian and how words go together. Last, but not least, you have a deeper understanding of the beliefs that inform hieroglyphic monuments. Now we can put these skills together to read a couple of celebrated inscriptions.

Marriage Inscription of Amenhotep III (*c.* 1390 BC)

Having read several kings' names, perhaps you are thinking it is all well and good to be able to do so, but how useful is it really? Well, we already noted that this is the commonest inscription associated with the pharaohs, found on monuments more often even than the offering formula. Of course, by reading the names you identify which pharaoh (or pharaohs) a monument is associated with. More than that, you have seen how the titularies of kings reveal fundamental beliefs about the divine nature of the king, about his relationships with gods and previous kings, about the extent of his authority, and about what tasks he actually carried out. However, still more can be learned. The king's titulary forms the basis of even the longest royal inscriptions, which, in turn, are among the most important historical sources to have survived from the ancient world. If you can read these royal inscriptions, you can learn a lot about our sources for ancient history.

How can a whole inscription be based on the king's name? Let us take a look at an example: an inscription of Amenhotep III, now in the Egyptian Museum in Cairo. The crucial historical inscriptions from the early reign of Amenhotep III (*c.* 1390–1353 BC) are stamped into the bottom of five different sets of large, glazed scarabs (beetle-shaped amulets) issued during his first 11 years as king. Over 200 are known from Egypt and abroad, from as far away as the Syrian port of Ugarit. The Cairo example measures 105 by 65 mm (4 x 2½ in.) across its inscribed face, and is 38 mm (1½ in.) deep.

41 Inscription of Amenhotep III naming his queen, Tiye, and her parents, Yuia and Tjuia.

Using our first principle of reading, begin with what you know. There are nine lines of hieroglyphs, but immediately you notice the cartouches in the centre. In line 4, the titles also show you that this is a king's name:

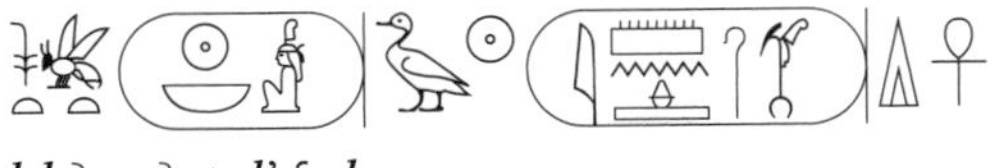 *nsw-bỉty nb-mꜣꜥt-rꜥ sꜣ rꜥ ỉmn-ḥtp-ḥkꜣ-wꜣst dỉ ꜥnḫ*

Dual king Nebmaatra, son of Ra Amenhotep-heqawast, given life (see page 98).

This, of course, is Amenhotep III, identified by his unique prenomen. There is another name in a cartouche in line 5, and the title tells you whose it is:

ḥmt-nsw tyy ꜥnḫ.ti͗
King's wife Tiye, living.

You met the word *ḥmt* 'wife' on pages 75 to 76, and, of course, her title is written with honorific transposition as *ḥmt-nsw* 'king's wife'. The epithet *ꜥnḫ.ti͗* 'living', which can often be found after the names of women, is a special form of *ꜥnḫ* 'live', but the grammar need not concern us here.

What matters is that you have found in the middle of this inscription a natural place around which to orientate your reading. So let us look at the rest in two parts: the inscription before these names, and the inscription after.

The first sign in line 1 is . This sign is typical at the start of any royal inscription, and you can perhaps understand it as a graphic device indicating that the king is 'live' or 'vital'. Like a cartouche, it has meaning (see page 86), but you do not need to translate it in words. Next you meet the title *ḥrw*, 'Horus', which indicates that this is the Horus name of the king. During the New Kingdom, every king had the phrase *kꜣ nḫt* 'strong bull' as part of his Horus-name (remember the imagery of the king as a bull on the label of Den above on page 120?), and then Amenhotep III has the unique addition *ḫꜥ-m-mꜣꜥt* 'Khammaat'. Now, if this is the Horus-name of the king and

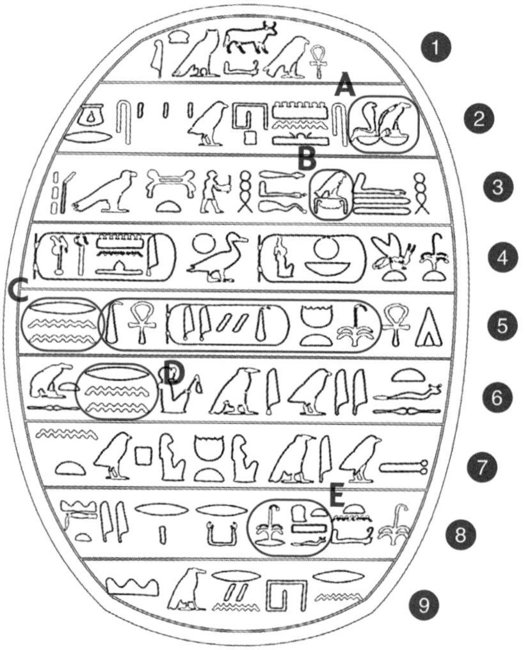

42 Inscription of Amenhotep III and Queen Tiye, with the inscription annotated.

his prenomen and nomen are in line 4, what lies between? The answer is, the rest of his name. By the end of the 3rd millennium BC, kings of Egypt had a complete titulary with *five names*, and this is what you see here. The two names you have not met before are as follows:

A The *twin-ladies name*, written after the title , which represents the southern vulture goddess *nḫbt* 'Nekhbet' together with the northern cobra goddess *wꜣḏyt* 'Wadjyt', both perched on the  *nb* sign. They are the goddesses who traditionally protect the king, and the title is usually read *nbty* 'twin ladies'.

B The *golden-falcon name*, introduced by the title , which represents a falcon perched on the word  *nbw* 'gold'. The title may read *bik nbw* 'falcon of gold' or *ḥrw nbw* 'Horus of gold'.

Neither of these names is usually written inside a special frame like the palace device or the cartouche. Because they are used infrequently on monuments, and because they are often complex, Egyptologists treat the twin-ladies name and golden-falcon name as statements to translate. There is a translation strategy you can use for this:

If you come across a word for an action (a verb) within a king's name, translate it using 'who does something'.

So, here you read as follows:

 *nbty smn hpw sgrḥ tꜣwy*

Twin ladies, who establishes laws, who calms the twin lands.

There are two words for actions in this name, 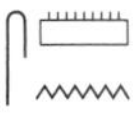 *smn* 'establish' and  *sgrḥ* 'calm', so within a name you translate 'who establishes' and 'who calms'. These are special forms of the words (called *participles*), but that is not important here. Just use your translation strategy above. Likewise, with the king's golden-falcon name:

 *bik nbw ꜥꜣ ḫpš ḥw stw*

Falcon of gold, great of strength, who strikes Asiatics.

Here we are told that the king is not merely *ꜥꜣ* 'great', but *ꜥꜣ ḫpš* 'great of strength'. Then his name includes the action *ḥw* 'strike', so you translate 'who strikes'. Let us recap the king's whole titulary, along with that of his queen:

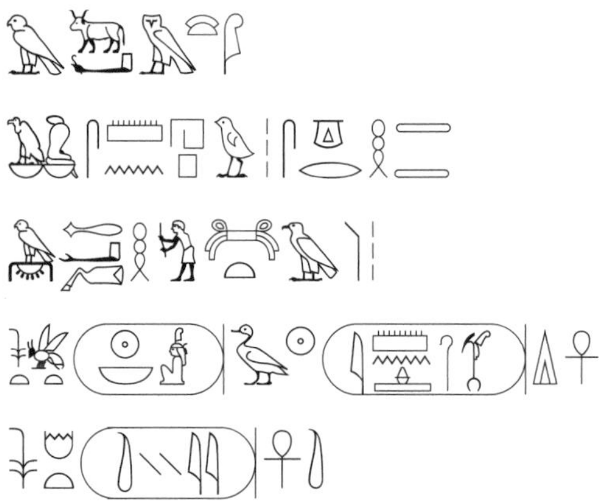

kꜣ nḫt ḫꜥ-m-mꜣꜥt Horus, strong bull, Khammaat,
nbty smn hpw sgrḥ tꜣwy Twin ladies, who establishes laws, who calms the twin lands,
bỉk nbw ꜥꜣ ḫpš ḥw stw Falcon of gold, great of strength, who strikes the Asiatics,
nsw bỉty nb-mꜣꜥt-rꜥ sꜣ rꜥ ỉmn-ḥtp-ḥkꜣ wꜣst Dual king Nebmaatra, son of Ra Amenhotep-heqawast, given life.
ḥmt-nsw tyy ꜥnḫ.tỉ The king's wife Tiye, living.

You see now that these names make up half the inscription. Which brings us to the second half, where appropriately enough we meet first the word *rn* 'name'. In fact it appears twice, at **C** and **D** in the phrase *rn n* 'the name of'. Whose names? Well, *rn n ỉt.s* 'the name of her father' and *rn n mwt.s* 'the name of her mother' (see page 75). (By the way, we can be sure from other inscriptions that writes *ỉt* 'father', although it seems to write *tf*. Writing or for *ỉt* 'father' is typical, see page 19.) So, after each of these phrases we expect names, and these are written out simply enough with 1-sound signs as *ywỉꜣ* (father) and *ṯwỉꜣ* (mother). So, to recap again we have a description of the queen, as follows:

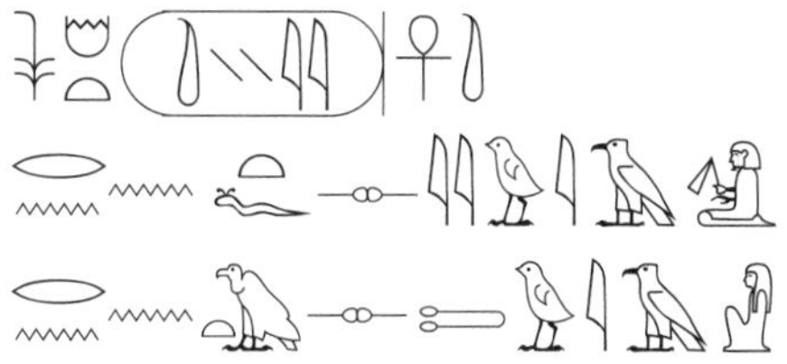

ḥmt-nsw tyy ꜥnḫ.tỉ 'The king's wife Tiye, living,'
rn n ỉt.s ywỉꜣ 'the name of her father, Yuia,'
rn n mwt.s ṯwỉꜣ 'the name of her mother, Tjuia.'

To finish reading this description of the queen you need to get to know a little, but very useful word, 𓊪𓅱 *-pw*.

#28 What You Need to Know: 𓊪𓅱 *-pw* 'he is' or 'she is'

The next part of the description of Queen Tiye reads as follows:

ḥmt -pw nt nsw nḫt

She is the wife of a strong king.

The basis of this statement is the phrase  *ḥmt -pw* 'she is the wife', in which 𓊪𓅱 *-pw* has the meaning 'she is'. Because 𓊪𓅱 *-pw* does not usually change its form, it may be translated 'he is', 'she is' or 'it is' depending on what the particular statement requires. This example also shows that 𓊪𓅱 *-pw*

DID YOU KNOW?

The many copies of this inscription are grouped together in our own history books as the Marriage Inscription or Marriage Scarab of Amenhotep III. In truth, it does not mention the act of marriage at all, although clearly the fact of the king's marriage to Tiye is important. This is a recurrent feature of ancient inscriptions: they often turn out to be something rather different than history books imply. This inscription is actually a statement about the king's authority, based on his titulary not his marriage. However, this sort of problem is no obstacle any more to you and your understanding of Ancient Egypt. You are getting to where you wish to be: you are beginning to read for yourself some of the most sophisticated and meaningful ancient inscriptions.

prefers to follow the first word in a statement, even if this means breaking up words that otherwise belong together, such as the phrase *ḥmt nt nsw nḫt* 'the wife of a strong king'. The need for words like *-pw* to follow another word (which is technically known as *dependency*) is shown in transliteration by using the hyphen.

Still, just when the inscription seems to have shifted from the king to the queen, you are brought back to where you started – the king. The final statement is based on the word *tꜣš.f* 'his boundary' in line 8 at **E**. Here it is part of the phrase *tꜣš.f rsy r kꜣry* 'his southern boundary at Karoy'. This statement about his southern boundary is followed by *mḥty r nhrynꜣ* 'the northern at Naharin'. In both of these statements the little word *r* means 'at' or 'towards'. You can put these statements together:

ḥmt -pw nt nsw nḫt

tꜣš.f rsy r kꜣry

mḥty r nhrynꜣ

She is the wife of a strong king,
his southern boundary at Karoy,
the northern at Naharin.

To the south (*rsy*), Karoy *kꜣry* was the region in northern Sudan beyond the fourth cataract on the Nile, the furthest along the river that Egyptians ever controlled. To the north (*mḥty*), Naharin *nhrynꜣ* means literally (in the Semitic languages) the land between 'the twin rivers', which are the Orontes and the Euphrates, in modern Syria. New Kingdom Egyptians used Naharin as a synonym for the kingdom of Mittani, with which Egyptians exchanged diplomatic gifts and fought wars. Therefore, this is the furthest extent north Egyptians controlled in ancient times. It is evidently in this sense that Tiye is the wife of *nsw nḫt* 'a *strong* king', and what we read about her actually tells us more about him.

Now practise what you have learned:

– the titulary of Amenhotep III
– □ 𓅱 'he is' and 'she is'
– more words used in royal inscriptions

Offering-Chapel of Sarenput II at Aswan (*c.* 1850 BC)

The rock-cut tombs of the governors of Elephantine are among the finest surviving from the Old and Middle Kingdoms. Their sizes and splendid decoration reflect the importance of the men who controlled the farthest edge of Egypt. This is the region of  *ḳbḥw* 'Water-spring', where the Nile emerges out of an almost intractable granite cataract to become the free-flowing highway of Egypt. Here the king marked his boundary in the living granite (see page 90). Beyond lay hostile deserts and the barely civilized (as the Egyptians understood it) tribes of the oases and Nubia. The value of the region for trade is reflected in the name  *ꜣbw* 'Elephantine', which literally means 'Ivory town' and may be written  instead. No other  *ḥꜣty-ꜥ* 'governor' was more valued by the king, nor more distant from the palace. The governor here was also responsible for maintaining the ancient cult of the ram-headed god  *ẖnmw* 'Khnum', who was titled  *nb-ḳbḥw* 'lord of Water-spring' and  *ḥry ꜣbw* 'chief of Elephantine', as well as the cult of his companion 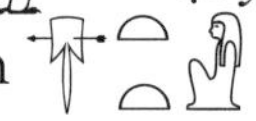 *stt* 'Satet', who was  *nbt-ꜣbw* 'lady of Elephantine'.

This is a cultural history of the far south of Egypt, and it is spelled out for you in the offering scene of Sarenput II (see opposite). Look at the scene and orientate yourself (see figure 44). You are familiar now with the image of the offering-table, so what of the inscription? In the centre of line 1 at **A** you see *reflected* the phrase 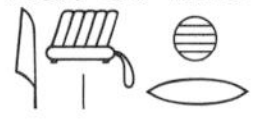 *imꜣḫw ḫr* 'revered one before', so there are *two inscriptions* reading in opposite directions. You expect the phrase 'revered one before' to be followed by the name of a god, so read to the left, where you can already notice Khnum's distinctive name at **B** and so anticipate his titles:

 *imꜣḫw ḫr ẖnmw nb-ḳbḥw ḥry ꜣbw*

revered one before Khnum, lord of Water-spring, chief of Elephantine

What follows on line 3 at **C** is the title  *ḥꜣty-ꜥ* 'governor', after which you expect to find the man's name.

43 Wall painting in the tomb of Sarenput II at Aswan.

Reading the inscription to the right you meet Satet at **D**, together with another goddess *nḫbt* ‘Nekhbet’ at **E**:

 *ỉmꜣḫw ḫr stt nbt-ꜣbw nḫbt*

revered one before Satet, lady of Elephantine, and Nekhbet

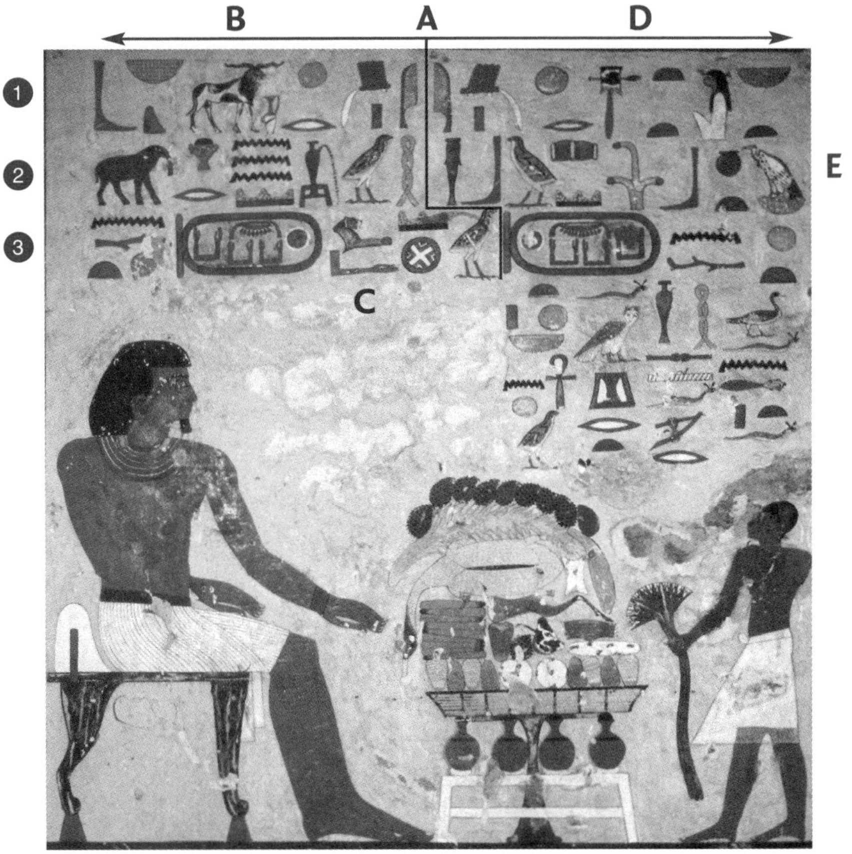

44 Text of Sarenput II with annotations.

This brings you again to line 3. All of this you have read using only your knowledge of the offering formula and your new-found understanding of the gods of Elephantine.

What is the man's name? You can see a cartouche repeated in the third line, but he is a governor not a king, so why a cartouche? The answer is that his name incorporates the name of a king, presumably the king in whose reign he was born or under whom he served. His name is  *nbw-kꜣw-rꜥ-nḫt* 'Nubkauranakht', which means 'Nubkaura is strong (*nḫt*)'. Nubkaura is the prenomen of Amenhotep II, which is why part of the man's name has been written in a cartouche (see page 138). Why is Sarenput the name at the head of this section? Well, the name Sarenput also appears in his tomb, so we may understand either Sarenput or Nubkauranakht as his birth-name and the other as the name he grew into (see page 46). Sarenput was also the name of his grandfather, whose tomb is nearby, so guidebooks about Aswan tend to refer to our man as Sarenput II. Anyway, Sarenput is an easier name to remember than Nubkauranakht.

Oddly enough, the hieroglyphs that form the man's name have been written using the correct orientation for the left and right inscriptions, but the two cartouches themselves have been written in the same direction. This creates the impression that line 3 is a single inscription, not the ends of two different inscriptions. This impression is emphasized by the fact that a line drawn down the middle of the scene separates the two inscriptions in the first two lines, but not in line 3. The artist has provided a clear visual cue at **A**, a natural starting point for our reading, that there are two separate inscriptions here, but then in line 3 he has tied them together visually, because the inscriptions belong together like the flip sides of a coin.

Think for a moment how much more visually complex this scene is than the stela of Mereri with which you began on page 10. Then reflect on how much knowledge and confidence you have gained since you began.

Finally, the artist has provided another visual cue, through the layout of the hieroglyphs, that there is a third inscription, which sits above the figure standing at the offering-table. From what you have learned already, you may presume that this is the son of the seated man (see **#21**). The hieroglyphs are there to confirm this.

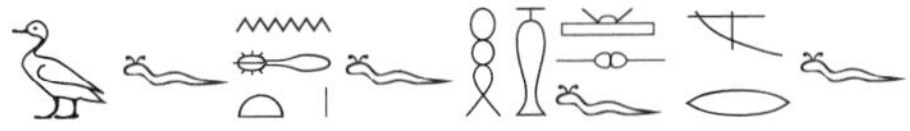

sꜣ.f n ẖt.f ḥss.f mrr.f

His son of his belly, whom he praises, whom he loves.

The phrase 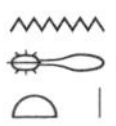 *n ẖt.f* 'of his belly' you have seen used of the king as son of the Sun-god (see page 110). The phrases  *ḥss.f* 'whom he

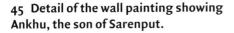

45 Detail of the wall painting showing Ankhu, the son of Sarenput.

praises' and *mrr.f* 'whom he loves' are special forms (known as relative forms), but you can learn them as set phrases because they are not uncommon in describing family members. Here they are qualified by another useful phrase: *m ẖrt nt rʿ nb* 'in the course (*ẖrt*) of every day' (the *n* of *nt* is missing in the photograph because the plaster has broken away). Finally, you learn that the son's name is *ʿnḫw* 'Ankhu'.

Now practise what you have learned:

– the offering text of Sarenput II

EPILOGUE

An Ancient Egyptian tomb is not only a burial place, it is a chapel for offerings. The largest tombs, like that of Sarenput II, quite obviously have the same form as the temples of the gods, including doorways inscribed with the owner's titles and name, and niches with statues and other images, such as the stelae and scenes you have read in this book. These chapels are areas intended for visitors, decorated for human eyes with traditional scenes and inscriptions. The burial chamber, however, was inaccessible at the bottom of a steep or vertical shaft, dropping maybe 3 or 4 m (10 to 13 ft) below the chapel's floor.

As you have learned, the heart of the offering cult is the relationship between the tomb owner and his son, which emulates the relationship between Osiris and Horus, and seeks to ensure the transmission of values across the generations (see **#21**). Because temples were inaccessible to most folk, ancestor worship and local festivals of the gods (often celebrated together) were the basic means for ancient Egyptians to come together in spiritual devotion and adoration (see **#19**). Meanwhile, in the burial chamber within the earth, the tomb owner has moved beyond the bounds of this life and the earthly relationships defined by his *kꜣ* (see **#17**). Instead, another aspect of the soul is prominent in the grave. Your *bꜣ* is that sense of yourself known only to you and your Creator. This sense of 'You' may seek to be part of the fabric of *mꜣꜥt*, to become *mꜣꜥ-ḫrw* 'true of voice', and to enter *dwꜣt* 'the state of adoration' alongside the gods. So now you understand from your own reading that the offering cult is a poignant and vivid statement about our mortal condition.

Now you know that reading hieroglyphs is invaluable, if you really seek to understand Ancient Egypt. For your next step, many (kindly) recommend a book I wrote with Mark Collier, *How To Read Egyptian Hieroglyphs* (British Museum, 2003). This deals briefly but intensively with the grammar you need to consolidate your comprehension. For a comprehensive grammar, seek out James P. Allen, *Introduction To Middle Egyptian* (Cambridge University, 2000), while the best dictionary in English is still Raymond Faulkner, *A Concise Dictionary of Middle Egyptian* (Griffith Institute, 1962).

LIST OF KINGS' NAMES

What follows is a list of names of kings of Egypt during the period covered by this book, roughly 3000 to 1100 BC (all dates given below are approximate). It concentrates on kings whose monuments you are most likely to encounter in museums or when visiting Egypt. Not every name of a king is given, only those most likely to help you recognize the king, while names in bold are those used in our history books. As a result, you will notice the shift from using Horus-names among the earliest kings to the combination of prenomen and nomen from the Old Kingdom onwards (see pages 84–87). Alongside each name below is a transliteration to help you with your reading, while signs you do not recognize can be found in the sign list beginning on page 144.

You may suppose that the kings whose monuments are grandest and most famous were the longest lived and most powerful. Sometimes, as with Ramesses II, that is undoubtedly the case, but often it is not. Other factors affect which monuments are known to us: one, of course, being archaeology. For example, among the earliest kings, the best attested are the 1st Dynasty because their cemetery at Abydos was discovered in the 19th century and has since been excavated on several occasions. By contrast, most royal tombs of the 2nd and 3rd Dynasties are only now being identified.

The names of kings in the 1st Dynasty are mostly aggressive, like Aha ('Fighter') or Den ('Crusher'). However, 2nd Dynasty names adopt a religious tone, such as Raneb ('The Sun is lord') and Ninetjer ('One belonging to God'). This religious tone remains typical for the remainder of the pharaonic period. The most famous name of the early period is the nomen 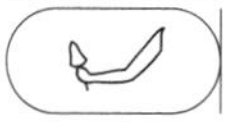 *ḏsr* Djoser ('Special one'), belonging to the king buried in the Step

Dynasties 1–3

1 (2950 BC)	**Narmer** (see page 114)		*nꜥrmr*
1	**Aha**		*ꜥḥꜣ*
1	**Djet** (see pages 84 and 118)		*ḏ*
1	**Den** (see page 119)	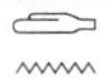	*dn*
1	**Qaa**		*ḳꜥ*
2 (2750 BC)	**Hetepsekhemwy**	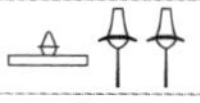	*ḥtpsḫmwy*
2	**Raneb** (see page 85)		*rꜥnb*
2	**Ninetjer**	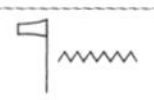	*nnṯr*
2	**Peribsen**		*prỉbsn*
2	**Khasekhemwy**	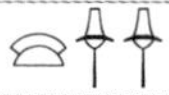	*ḫꜥsḫmwy*
3 (2650 BC)	Netjerkhet **Djoser**	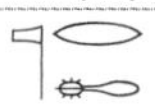	*nṯrḫt*  *ḏsr*

Pyramid at Saqqara. However, this name was given to him in much later tradition, and he was known during his lifetime by the Horus-name Netjerkhet ('God by flesh').

Sometimes a single monument defines our understanding of a particular king. Hence Khufu is celebrated as the builder of the Great Pyramid at Giza, one of the wonders of the ancient world, but little else has survived from his reign. Indeed, several of the kings named on this page are known by and large only from their burials. Of course, another factor affecting the survival of monuments is the sheer length of time since these kings lived. The sites of their palaces and temples might have been reused many times in the intervening millennia until only their tombs were left. With many Old Kingdom rulers, you may find their names written more often in the burials of the officials who served them in life and the priests who served them in death than in standing royal monuments. A case in point is Pepy II, the longest-reigning monarch in human history, with an astonishing 94 years on the throne of Horus. None the less, the thin scatter of his surviving monuments no longer offers a clear and consistent picture of his reign.

Dynasties 4–10

4 (2575 BC)	**Snefru**	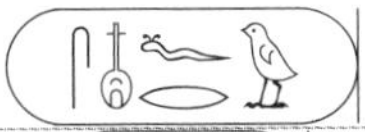	*snfrw*		
4	**Khufu**		*ḫwfw*		
4	**Djedefra**	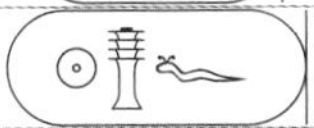	*ḏdfrʿ*		
4	**Khafra**	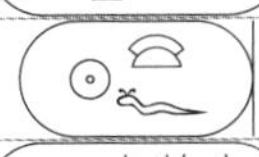	*ḫʿfrʿ*		
4	**Menkaura**	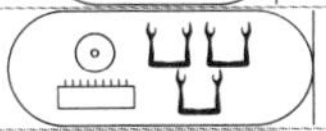	*mnkꜣwrʿ*		
4	**Shepseskaf**		*špsskꜣf*		
5 (2450 BC)	**Sahura**		*sꜣḥwrʿ*		
5	**Neferirkara** Kakai	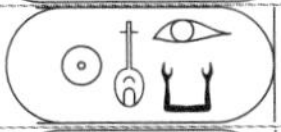	*nfrỉrkꜣrʿ*		*kꜣkꜣỉ*
5	Djedkara **Isesi**	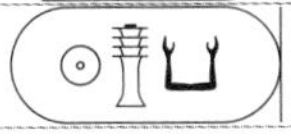	*ḏdkꜣrʿ*	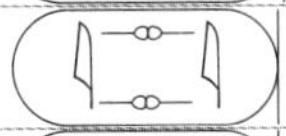	*ỉssỉ*
5	**Unas**				*wnỉs*
6 (2325 BC)	**Teti**				*ttỉ*
6	Meryra **Pepy I**	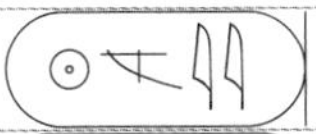	*mryrʿ*		*ppy*
6	**Merenra**		*mrnrʿ*		
6	Neferkara **Pepy II** (2270–2175)	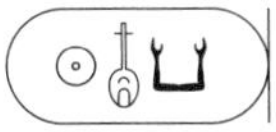	*nfrkꜣrʿ*		*ppy*
10 (2100 BC)	Meryibra **Khety**	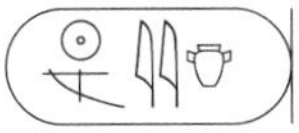	*mryỉbrʿ*	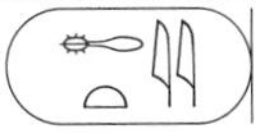	*ḫty*

Dynasties 11–15

Dyn.	King				
11	Nebhepetra **Montjuhotep (II)** (2010–1960)	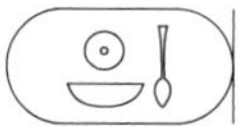	*nbḥptrˁ*		*mnṯwḥtp*
11	Sankhara **Montjuhotep (III)** (1960–1948)	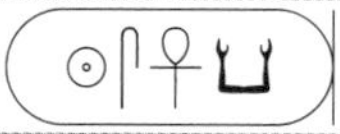	*sˁnḫkꜣrˁ*		*mnṯwḥtp*
12	Sehetepibra **Amenemhat (I)** (1938–1908)	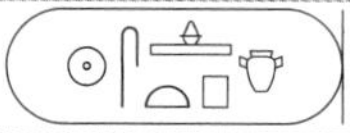	*sḥtpỉbrˁ*		*ỉmnmḥꜣt*
12	Kheperkara **Senusret (I)** (1918–1875)		*ḫprkꜣrˁ*	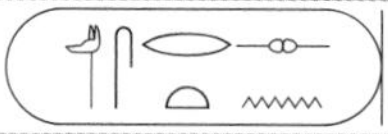	*snwsrt*
12	Nubkaura **Amenemhat (II)** (1876–1842, see page 132)	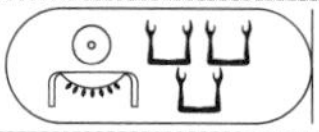	*nbwkꜣwrˁ*		*ỉmnmḥꜣt*
12	Khakheperra **Senusret (II)** (1842–1837)	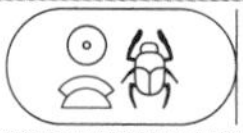	*ḫˁḫprrˁ*	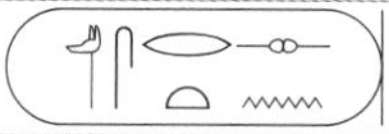	*snwsrt*
12	Khakaura **Senusret (III)** (1836–1818, see page 86)		*ḫˁkꜣwrˁ*	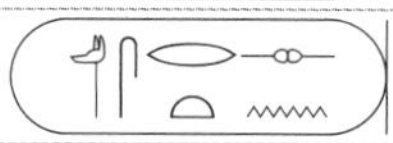	*snwsrt*
12	Nimaatra **Amenemhat (III)** (1818–1870)	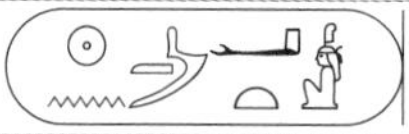	*nmꜣˁtrˁ*	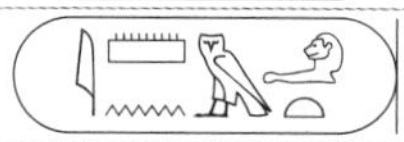	*ỉmnmḥꜣt*
13	Auibra **Her**	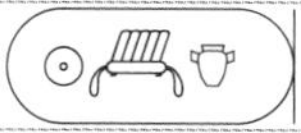	*ꜣwỉbrˁ*		*ḥrw*
13	Userkara **Khendjer**		*wsrkꜣrˁ*		*ḫnḏr*
13	Khasekhemra **Neferhotep**		*ḫˁsḫmrˁ*	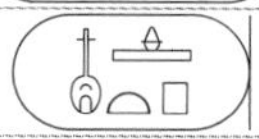	*nfrḥtp*
13	Khaneferra **Sobkhotep**	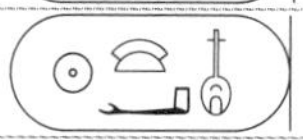	*ḫˁnfrrˁ*		*sbkḥtp*
15	Suserenra **Khyan**	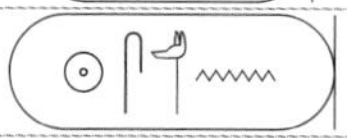	*swsrnrˁ*		*ḫyꜣn*
15	Auserra Apepi (=**Apophis**) (1570–1530)	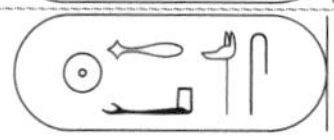	*ˁꜣwsrrˁ*		*ỉppỉ*

The Middle Kingdom is founded on two families: the 11th Dynasty, many of whom had the nomen Montjuhotep; and the 12th Dynasty, in which you see the alternate nomens Amenemhat and Senusret. Notice also how their prenomens, although unique to each king, show a thematic development. For example, from Senusret I to Senusret III the prenomens use variations on the words  *kꜣ* 'soul',  *ḫpr* 'happen' and  *ḫˁ* 'appear'. Kings of the 13th Dynasty are much less well known to historians and their nomens or family names are more random, but you see the same words often still used in their prenomens, along with new themes such as the word  *wsr* 'power'. Apparently the prenomen of a new king was composed in part by looking back at the stated identities of his predecessors. Notice also that the 15th Dynasty kings, who are frequently treated by historians and by some ancient sources as foreign (the so-called Hyksos), evidently saw themselves as traditional Egyptian kings and devised their prenomens accordingly.

Dynasties 17–18

17	Wadjkheperra **Kamose**-nakht (1541–1539)	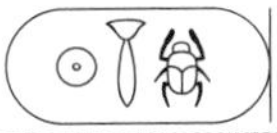	*wꜣḏḫprrꜥ*		*kꜣms-nḫt*
18	Nebpehtyra **Ahmose** (1539–1514)		*nbpḥtyrꜥ*		*iꜥḥms*
18	Djeserkara **Amenhotep (I)** (1514–1493)		*ḏsrkꜣrꜥ*	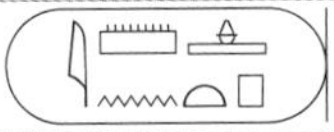	*imnḥtp*
18	Aakheperkara **Thutmose (I)** (1493–1481)		*ꜥꜣḫprkꜣrꜥ*	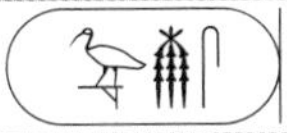	*ḏḥwtyms*
18	Aakheperenra **Thutmose (II)** (1481–1479)	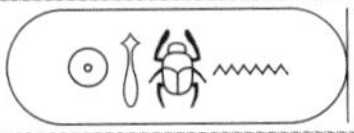	*ꜥꜣḫprnrꜥ*		*ḏḥwtyms*
18	Menkheperra **Thutmose (III)** (1479–1425)	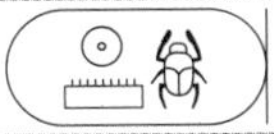	*mnḫprrꜥ*		*ḏḥwtyms*
18	Maatkara **Hatshepsut**-khnemetamen (1473–1458)	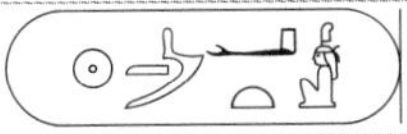	*mꜣꜥtkꜣrꜥ*		*ḥꜣtšpswt-ḫnmt-imn*
18	Aakheperura **Amenhotep (II)**-netjerheqaiunu (1426–1400)	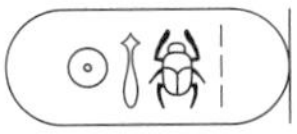	*ꜥꜣḫprwrꜥ*	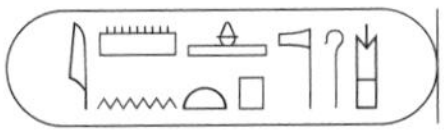	*imnḥtp-nṯrḥkꜣwnw*
18	Menkheprura **Thutmose (IV)**-khakau (1400–1390, see page 97)	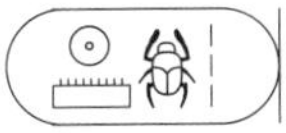	*mnḫprwrꜥ*	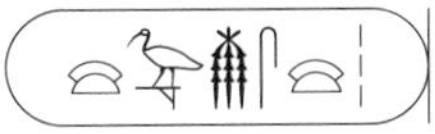	*ḏḥwtyms-ḫꜥḫꜥw*
18	Nebmaatra **Amenhotep (III)**-netjerheqawast (1390–1353, see page 122)		*nbmꜣꜥtrꜥ*	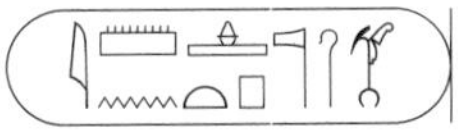	*imnḥtp-nṯrḥkꜣwꜣst*
18	Neferkheperura-waenra **Akhenaten** (1353–1336)	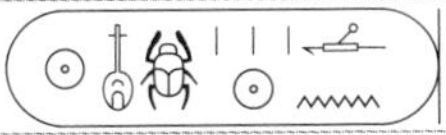	*nfrḫprwrꜥ-wꜥnrꜥ*		*ꜣḫnitn*
18	Ankheprura **Smenkhkara**-djeserkhepru (1336–1332)		*ꜥnḫḫprwrꜥ*		*smnḫkꜣrꜥ-ḏsrḫprw*
18	Nebkheperura **Tutankhamun**-heqaiunushema (1332–1322, see page 107)	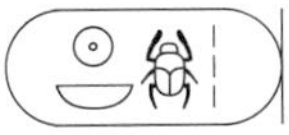	*nbḫprwrꜥ*		*twtꜥnḫimn-ḥkꜣwnwšmꜣ*
18	Kheperkheprura-irmaat Itnetjer-**Ay**-heqawast (1322–1319)	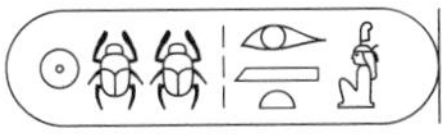	*ḫprḫprwrꜥ-irmꜣꜥt*		*itnṯr-iy-ḥkꜣwꜣst*
18	Djeserkheprura-setepenra **Horemheb**-merenamun (1319–1292)		*ḏsrḫprwrꜥ-stpnrꜥ*		*ḥrmḥb-mrnimn*

During the first 250 years of the New Kingdom, Egypt was ruled by one family, reflected again in the alternation of the nomens Amenhotep and Thutmose. (In fact, we know of other Amenhoteps and Thutmoses born into this family who did not live long enough to become king.) Likewise, themes are apparent in devising their prenomens. Early on, using the word  *kꜣ* seems to look back to the Middle Kingdom, but the word  *ḫpr* 'happen' becomes especially prominent. Eventually, every king but one from

Dynasties 19–20

19	Menpehtyra **Ramesses (I)** (1292–1290)		*mnpḥtyrˁ*	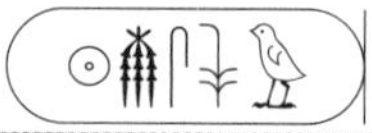	*rˁmssw*
19	Menmaatra **Sety (I)**-merenptah (1290–1279)		*mnm3ˁtrˁ*		*sty-mrnptḥ*
19	Usermaatra-setepenra **Ramesses (II)**-meramun (1279–1213, see page 92)		*wsrm3ˁtrˁ-stpnrˁ*	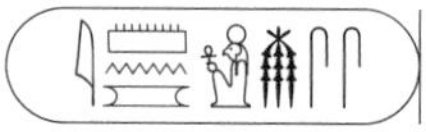	*rˁmssw-mrỉmn*
19	Baenra-merynetjeru **Merenptah**-hetephirmaat (1213–1204)	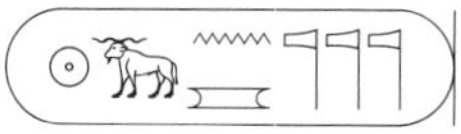	*b3nrˁ-mryntrw*	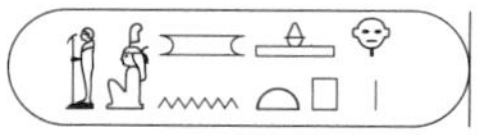	*mrnptḥ-ḥtpḥrm3ˁt*
19	Userkheperura-setepenra **Sety (II)**-merenptah (1204–1198)	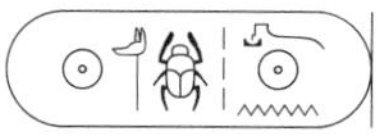	*wsrḫprwrˁ-stpnrˁ*		*sty-mrnptḥ*
20	Usermaatra-meramun **Ramesses (III)**-netjer-heqaiunu (1187–1156)		*wsrm3ˁtrˁ-mryỉmn*	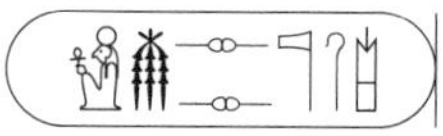	*rˁmssw-ntrḥk3iwnw*
20	Heqamaatra **Ramesses (IV)** (1156–1150)		*ḥk3m3ˁtrˁ*	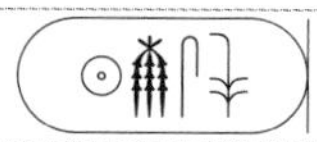	*rˁmssw*
20	Nebmaatra-meramun **Ramesses (VI)**-netjerheqaiunu (1145–1137)		*nbm3ˁtrˁ-mryỉmn*	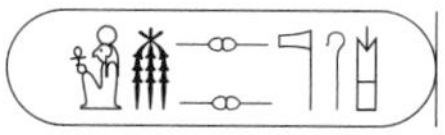	*rˁmssw-ntrḥk3iwnw*
20	Neferkara-setepenra **Ramesses (IX)**-khawast-mereramun (1126–1108)	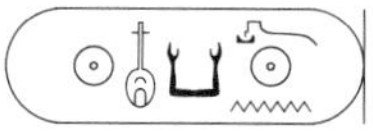	*nfrk3rˁ-stpnrˁ*	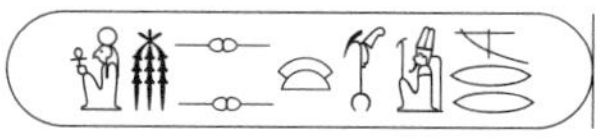	*rˁmssw-ḫˁw3st-mrrỉmn*

Amenhotep II until the end of the dynasty had a prenomen of the form  *?-ḫprwrˁ*, in which only one element (= ?) is different in each case. Much is made in our history books of the radical, even iconoclastic, innovations of Akhenaten in monumental art, but his prenomen sits easily on this list. From Thutmose III epithets become an increasingly common complication within cartouches (see page 101).

A third factor affecting the survival of monuments becomes apparent at this time. Often the amount of monumental building undertaken by kings is related more to the number of jubilee-festivals a king celebrated than to the actual length of his reign. Of course, the longer a king reigned the more jubilees he would likely celebrate. However, some kings, such as Amenhotep I and Akhenaten, celebrated an unusually high number of jubilees and so have left disproportionately more monuments than other kings who might have reigned longer, such as Amenhotep II.

The list for the later New Kingdom is dominated by the nomen Ramesses. Notice that the first Ramesses, head of a new dynasty, looked back to Ahmose, the head of the previous dynasty, to get the model for his prenomen. The most famous king in Egypt's history is Ramesses II, who built many of the grandest ancient temples still standing.

One element of his prenomen *wsrmꜣꜥtrꜥ* is the original source of the name of Shelley's *Ozymandias*. However, his father, Sety I, and son, Merenptah, were also prodigious builders, while in the next dynasty his namesake Ramesses III was of the same ilk. Other kings of the era are less celebrated in history but their tombs in the Valley of the Kings remain among the grandest spectacles of Egypt. Cartouches of this era are usually complicated by the use of epithets, especially *stpnrꜥ* 'one whom the Sun has chosen' and *mry ỉmn* 'beloved of Amun' (see pages 92–96).

LIST OF GODS

This is your check-list for the names and titles of the gods you have met in this book. No book could give a complete list of the gods of Ancient Egypt because there is literally no limit to their number. The gods constitute something akin to a language of divinity, and they are no more limited than the words of a language. New gods may be devised, foreign gods adopted, and two or three or more gods combined to create a meaning distinct from the sum of its parts. Conversely, the same god may appear in different forms and use different titles on different monuments.

None the less, there are consistent beliefs. The first of these is the principle that this world has not come about randomly but is happening through the *will* of a Creator. In other words, there is intention and meaning inherent in everything, which we humans respond to. The Egyptian word for this principle is *mꜣꜥt* 'Maat' (see page 57). The Creator may be called *tmw* 'Atum = Non-Being', or identified through various names, including some noted below. A traditional analogy for the Creator especially relevant to your reading here is the presence of *rꜥ* 'Ra = the Sun'. The Sun brings energy and illumination, marks the passage of time, and allows the possibility of life. However, in a desert country such as Egypt, it has power beyond any earthly authority to exterminate and erase all that has been created. Hence the Sun is an obvious indication of a wilful power greater than any earthly authority, although the kingship exists to allow that heavenly power to guide civilized life on earth.

The first king, *ꜣsỉr* 'Osiris', was the first man to die, and his titles reflect his story (see page 53 and **#20**):

nṯr ꜥꜣ	'the great god'
nb-ḏdw	'lord of Djedu'
nb-ꜣbḏw	'lord of Abydos'
nb-tꜣ ḏsr	'lord of the sacred land' (see page 111)
ḫnty ỉmntw	'foremost of the westerners'
ḥḳꜣ nṯrw	'ruler of the gods'
nb-pt	'lord of the sky'

A god closely associated with Osiris is the funerary god  *ỉnpw* 'Anubis', whom you have met with these titles:

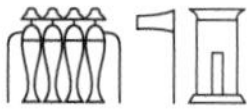	*ḫnt sḥ-nṯr* 'in front at the god's booth'	An Ancient Egyptian shrine was approached on a straight line from the entrance, so the god would literally be in front of any worshipper as well as pre-eminent in importance.
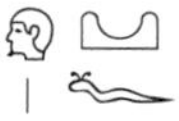	*tp ḏw.f* 'upon his hill'	Anubis is identified with burial and cemeteries, hence he is shown as a wild or feral dog, glimpsed on the margins of communities in the twilight.

Anubis' other typical titles include:

	*ỉmy wt* 'who is in the *ut*'	*ut* seems to be a fetish used in shrines of Anubis, probably related to evisceration while embalming.
	*nb-tꜣ ḏsr* 'lord of the sacred land'	A title shared with Osiris and other funerary gods, especially associated with Abydos (see page 111).

Some other gods you have met play parts in the story of Osiris:

	Horus *ḥrw*	The son of Osiris defeated his father's killer, and took the throne in his place. Each new king becomes the incarnation of Horus, whose own sons, including  *dwꜣmwtf* 'Duamutef' (see pages 79–80), protect the dead.
	Isis *ꜣst*	The wife of Osiris embalmed his dismembered body, allowing him to attain the state of adoration. She was then able to conceive Horus, and raise him in hiding from his enemies.
	*nbt-pt* 'mistress of the sky'	Despite the transcendence of her title here, Isis is a sympathetic figure – wife, widow and mother.
	Geb *gb*	The earth, which engendered Osiris. The physical body is returned to Geb in the tomb. The interaction of Geb and Nut engenders all physical creation.
	Nut *nwt*	The sky, which gave birth to Osiris. Nut is often shown inside coffins giving birth to the deceased, but in the guise of the starry sky into which the soul of the deceased is freed.
	Shu *šw*	In the first act of creation, the Egyptian Creator spoke the word *šw* 'light', just as in St John's Gospel. The interaction of Shu and Tefnut, as male and female, gave form to creation as the earth (Geb) and sky (Nut).
	Tefnut *tfnwt*	The female counterpart of Shu is the moisture of the atmosphere. She is the female principal through whom reproduction became possible.

You have met several other major gods:

Amun	*ỉmn*	A name of the Creator. He had many temples, especially in Thebes and Nubia. From the Middle Kingdom, the king was closely associated with Amun.	
Hathor	*ḥtḥr*	A goddess associated with the power of women, including sexuality and childbirth. She may appear as a cosmic force or simply as a household guardian.	*nbt-nht* 'lady of the sycamore'
Khnum	*ẖnmw*	A name of the Creator. His temple at Elephantine is known back to prehistoric times (see page 103).	*nb-ḳbḥw* 'lord of Water-spring' *ḥry ꜣbw* 'chief of Elephantine'
Nekhbet	*nḫbt*	Goddess of the far south of Egypt, her principal temple was in El-Kab.	Identified also with the name *nbty* 'twin ladies' (see page 125)
Ptah	*ptḥ*	A name of the Creator. He had many temples at Memphis and elsewhere, and was closely associated with the king, burial and craftsmanship.	
Satet	*sṯt*	Associated with Khnum, she represents taming the desert.	*nbt-ꜣbw* 'lady of Elephantine'
Seshat	*sšꜣt*	The deification of writing, she implies authority rather than education.	*nbt-sẖ* 'lady of writing'
Sokar	*skr*	God of the necropolis of Saqqara, closely identified with Ptah.	
Wadjyt	*wꜣḏyt*	Goddess of the far north of Egypt, her principal temple was in Buto.	Identified also with the name *nbty* 'twin ladies' (see page 125)

The following gods appear in this book only as part of a person's name:

Min	*mnw*	A name of the Creator, with his principal temple in Coptos. Associated especially with the fertility of crops.
Montju	*mnṯw*	Associated especially with the warlike aspect of the kingship, his principal temple was at Armant.

Sobk		*sbk*	A name of the Creator, with several temples in the Faiyum region and elsewhere.
Usret		*wsrt*	A name meaning 'powerful one', she may be a distinct deity or a euphemism for a goddess such as Hathor.
Thoth		*ḏḥwty*	Associated with the moon, learning and understanding what is obscure, his principal temple was at Ashmunein.

LIST OF HIEROGLYPHIC SIGNS

The following is a list of all the hieroglyphs in this book, with an explanation of how each one has been used to write words. You can also treat it as a convenient resource for memorizing some commonly used hieroglyphs, along with the tables on pages 11–12, 18–19, 24–25 and 27–28. In order to help you identify hieroglyphs quickly and easily, the signs in this list have been divided into six broad categories. More recognizable signs have been grouped into three categories (humans, creatures, nature), while the others have been grouped by shape (small, tall, broad). The forms of the signs given here are standardized, but remember that there is bound to be some variation in the form of a sign as it actually appears in any inscription, where it may be carved or painted in some detail.

This list is only intended for use with this book. Readers who wish to continue their study of Egyptian will eventually need to become familiar with the standard sign list used in Sir Alan Gardiner's magisterial *Egyptian Grammar* (Griffith Institute, 1957) and more recently also in Allen's *Middle Egyptian* (see page 135). However, the standard list uses many more signs and categories than are useful here, so there is no correspondence between this list and Gardiner's list. However, the code used in Gardiner's list is given at the end of each description below.

The following abbreviations have been used: 1s. = 1-sound sign; 2s. = 2-sound sign; 3s. = 3-sound sign; det. = determinative; abb. = abbreviation; com. = sign combined with other elements. Signs marked with an asterix* are listed in more than one place.

§A Signs depicting people or parts of the human body

A1 A2 A3 A4 A5 A5* A6 A7 A8* A9* A10

A11 A12 A13 A14 A15 A16 A17 A18 A19 A20 A21

A22 A23 A24 A25 A26 A27 A28 A29 A30*

§B Signs depicting creatures or parts of their bodies

B1 B2 B3 B4 B5 B6 B7 B8 B9 B10 B11 B12
B13 B14 B15 B16 B17 B18 B19 B20 B21 B22 B23* B24
B25 B26 B27 B28 B29 B30 B31 B32* B33 B34 B35 B36*
B37 B38 B39 B40 B41 B42 B43 A8* A9* A30* E37*

§C Signs involving sky, earth, water, or plants

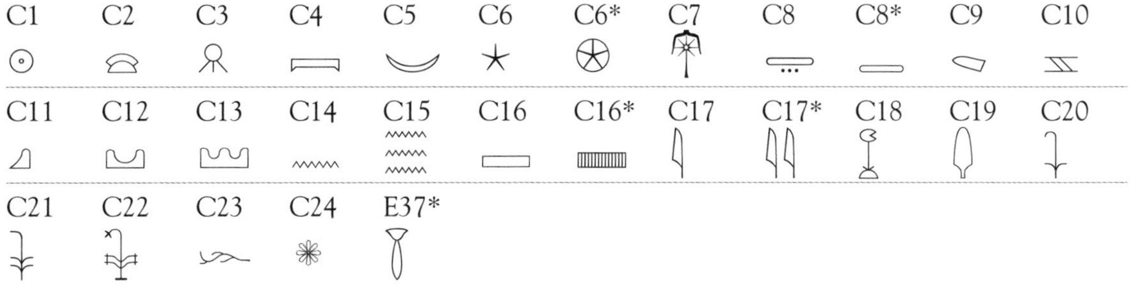
C1 C2 C3 C4 C5 C6 C6* C7 C8 C8* C9 C10
C11 C12 C13 C14 C15 C16 C16* C17 C17* C18 C19 C20
C21 C22 C23 C24 E37*

§D Other small signs

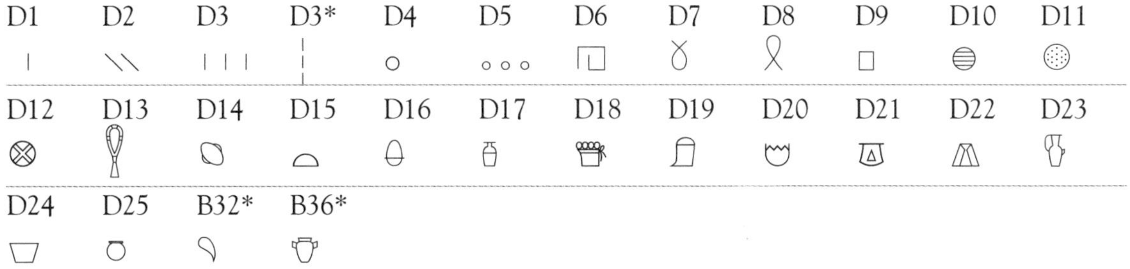
D1 D2 D3 D3* D4 D5 D6 D7 D8 D9 D10 D11
D12 D13 D14 D15 D16 D17 D18 D19 D20 D21 D22 D23
D24 D25 B32* B36*

§E Other tall signs

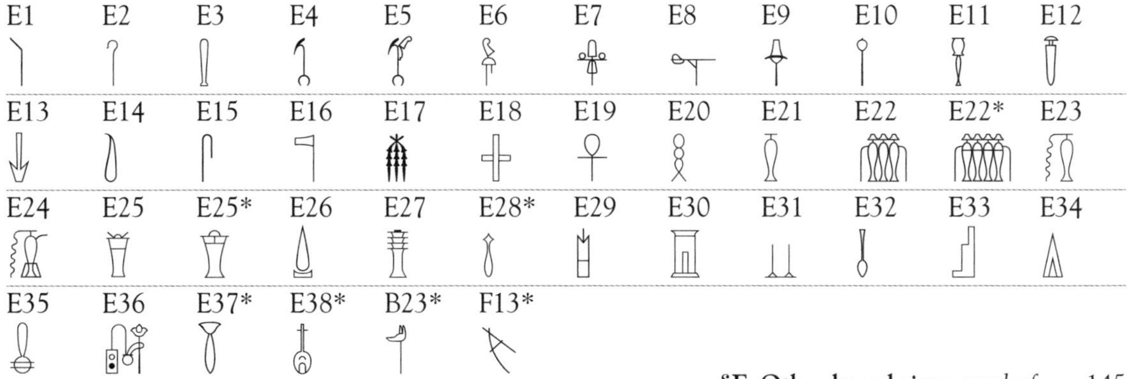
E1 E2 E3 E4 E5 E6 E7 E8 E9 E10 E11 E12
E13 E14 E15 E16 E17 E18 E19 E20 E21 E22 E22* E23
E24 E25 E25* E26 E27 E28* E29 E30 E31 E32 E33 E34
E35 E36 E37* E38* B23* F13*

§F Other broad signs *overleaf*

§F Other broad signs

F1*	F2	F3	F4	F5	F5*	F6	F7	F8	F9	F10
F11	F12	F13*	F14	F15	F16	F17	F18	F19	F20	F21
F22	F23	F25	F26	F27	F28	F29	F30			

FULL SIGN LIST

Codes in square brackets refer to Gardiner's sign list

§A Signs depicting people or parts of the human body

A1		man seated	det. man, occupations of men [A1]
A2		man with hand to mouth	(1) det. speaking (2) in for initial *ỉ* [A2]
A3		woman seated	det. woman, occupations of women [B1]
A4		god seated	det. god, titles of gods [A40]
A5		goddess with feather on head	det. or abb. *mꜣꜥt* 'order' [C10]
A5*		A5 com. E19	variant of A4
A6		seated shepherd	det. or abb. *sꜣw* 'guardian' [A47]
A7		man kneeling with flail	det. dignitary, deceased [A52]
A8*		god Seth	det. or abb. *stẖ* '(the god) Seth' [C7]
A9*		sun-god	det. or abb. *rꜥ* '(the god) Ra' or another sun-god [C2]
A10		god Amun	det. or abb. *ỉmn* '(the god) Amun' [C12]
A11		god Ptah	det. or abb. *ptḥ* '(the god) Ptah' [C20]
A12		face in frontal view	2s. *ḥr* [D2]
A13		head in profile view	2s. *tp* [D1]
A14		eye	2s. *ỉr* [D4]
A15		mouth	1s. *r* [D21]
A16		hand	1s. *d* [D46]

A17		arm with palm up	(1) 1s. *ꜥ* (2) variant of A17 [D36]
A18		arm com. E34	(1) 2s. *di͗* or 1s. *d* (2) abb. *rdi͗* 'give' [D37]
A19		arm holding bread	2s. *mi͗* or 1s. *m* [D38]
A20		arm holding stick	variant of A25 [D40]
A21		arm with palm down	det. action with arm, calm [D41]
A22		arm holding lettuce	3s. *ḏsr* [D45]
A23		D25 pouring water com. A27	3s. *wꜥb* [D60]
A24		man with arms raised	det. high in the word *ḳꜣ* 'high', used to write part of the name *ḳꜣi͗t* [A28]
A25		raised arms	2s. *kꜣ* [D28]
A26		man striking with stick	(1) det. force (2) abb. *nḫt* 'strong' [A24]
A27		arms holding shield and axe	abb. *ꜥḥꜣ* 'fight' and related words [D34]
A28		lower leg	1s. *b* [D58]
A29		walking legs com. D22	2s. *i͗n* [W25]
A30*		human-headed bird with brazier	abb. *bꜣ* 'soul' [G53]

§B Signs depicting creatures or parts of their bodies

B1		quail chick	1s. *w* [G43]
B2		owl	1s. *m* [G17]
B3		Egyptian vulture	1s. *ꜣ* [G1]
B4		buzzard	2s. *tw*, often confused with B3 [G4]
B5		pintail duck	(1) 2s. *sꜣ* (2) det. bird, alternative for B6 [G39]
B6		goose	(1) 2s. *gb* (2) det. bird [G38]
B7		duck's head	abb. *ꜣpd* 'fowl' [H1]
B8		falcon	(1) det. falcon (2) abb. *ḥrw* '(the god) Horus' [G5]
B9		B8 com. F26	*bi͗k nbw*; part of the king's titulary [G8]
B10		B8 com. temple	abb. *ḥtḥr* '(the goddess) Hathor' [O10]
B11		vulture	3s. *mwt* or 2s. *mt* [G14]

B12		B11 and cobra com. F3	*nbty*; part of the king's titulary [G16]
B13		Ibis com. E8	abb. *ḏḥwty* '(the god) Thoth' [G26]
B14*		B8 com. E8	det. or abb. *ỉmnt* 'the west' and related words [R13]
B15		feather	(1) 2s. *šw* (2) det. or abb. *mꜣꜥt* 'order' [H6]
B16		bull	det. or abb. bull, cattle [E1]
B17		bull's head	abb. *kꜣ* 'ox/bull' [F1]
B18		elephant	abb. *ꜣbw* 'Elephantine island' [E26]
B19		ram	det. or abb. *ẖnmw* '(the god) Khnum' [E10]
B20		kid	2s. *ỉb* [E8]
B21		hare	2s. *wn* [E34]
B22		dog on shrine	det. or abb. *ỉnpw* '(the god) Anubis' [E16]
B23*		dog's head on oar (?)	3s. *wsr* [F12]
B24		forepart of lion	3s. *ḥꜣt* [F4]
B25		head of leopard	(1) 2s. *pḥ* (2) as  for *pḥty* 'strength' [F9]
B26		leg of bull	3s. *ḫpš* [F23]
B27		leg of ox	3s. *wḥm* [F25]
B28		animal belly with tail	1s. *ẖ* [F32]
B29		skin pierced with arrow	2s. *sṯ* or *st* [F29]
B30		ox ear	3s. *ỉdn* [F21]
B31		gazelle horns	3s. *ỉḥs* or 2s. *ỉs* in the name  *ỉsw* 'Yesu'
B32*		piece of flesh	det. *ꜣst* '(the goddess) Isis' [F51]
B33		ox tongue	abb. *m-r* 'overseer' [F20]
B34		spine with issue of marrow	3s. *mꜣẖ* [F39]
B35		spine with further issue of marrow	2s. *ꜣw* [F40]
B36*		heart	det. or abb. *ỉb* 'heart' [F34]
B37		bulti (fish)	2s. *ỉn* [K1]
B38		catfish	3s. *nꜥr*

B39		cobra	1s. *ḏ* [I10]
B40		viper	(1) 1s. *f* (2) det. *ỉt* 'father' (see page 19) [I9]
B41		mummified crocodile	det. or abb. *sbk* '(the god) Sobk' [I5]
B42		beetle	3s. *ḫpr* [L1]
B43		bee	(1) 3s. *bỉt* (2) abb. *bỉty* 'king' [L2]

§C Signs involving sky, earth, water or plants

C1		sun-disc	det. or abb. *rꜥ* 'day' or '(the god) Ra' [N5]
C2		sunrise above hills	2s. *ḫꜥ* [N28]
C3		sun with sunlight	det. *šw* 'sunlight' or '(the god) Shu' [N8]
C4		canopy of the sky	det. or abb. *pt* 'sky' [N1]
C5		moon	det. or abb. *ỉꜥḥ* 'moon' [N11]
C6		star	3s. *dwꜣ* [N14]
C6*		C6 com. globe	det. or abb. *dwꜣt* 'adoration' [N15]
C7		standard of goddess Seshat	det. or abb. *sšꜣt* '(the goddess) Seshat' [R20]
C8		strip of land com. D5	(1) abb. *tꜣ* 'land'; (2) 2s. *tꜣ* [N16]
C8*		variant of C8	variant of C8 [N17]
C9		tongue of land	det. land [N21]
C10		irrigation channels	det. irrigated land [N23]
C11		slope of hill	1s. *ḳ* [N29]
C12		valley between hills	2s. *ḏw* [N26]
C13		desert hills	det. desert [N25]
C14		ripple of water	1s. *n* [N35]
C15		group of ripples	(1) det. water (2) 2s. *mw* [N35]
C16	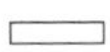	garden pool	(1) det. or abb. lake (2) 1s. *š* [N37]
C16*		variant of C16	variant of C16 [N39]
C17		reed	1s. *ỉ* [M17]
C17*		pair of reeds	1s. *y* [M17]
C18		lotus	(1) 2s. *ḫꜣ*; (2) abb. *ḫꜣ* 'thousand', or units of thousands in counting [M12]

C19	tree	det. tree [M1]
C20	rush	3s. *nḫb* [M22]
C21	sedge plant	(1) 2s. *sw* (2) abb. *nsw* 'king' [M23]
C22	flowering sedge	abb. or det. *šmʿ* 'Upper Egypt' [M26]
C23	tree branch	2s. *ḫt* [M3]
C24	rosette	reading uncertain (see page 115)

§D Other small signs

D1	single stroke	forms a word group (see **#13**) [Z1]
D2	pair of strokes	1s. *y* [Z4]
D3	three strokes	det. groups or collections, or sometimes plurals (see **#24**) [Z2]
D3*	variant of D3	variant of D3 [Z3]
D4	grain of sand	det. mineral [N33]
D5	grains of sand	(1) variant of D5 (2) rarely as variant of D3 [N33]
D6	reed shelter	1s. *h* [O4]
D7	twisted cord	2s. *šs* [V6]
D8	twisted cord	2s. *šn* [V7]
D9	reed mat or stool	1s. *p* [Q3]
D10	ball of twine	1s. *ḫ* [Aa1]
D11	threshing-floor with grain	2s. *sp* [O50]
D12	roads within enclosure	det. community [O49]
D13	portable enclosure	(1) det. protection (2) det. tent [V18]
D14	pustule	det. cleansing, hence (?) det. in writing the *wt*-fetish of Anubis [Aa2]
D15	bun	1s. *t* [X1]
D16	small loaf	det. or abb. *t* 'bread' [X2]
D17	beer jug	det. or abb. *ḥnḳt* 'beer' [W22]
D18	bundle of flax	2s. *ḏr* [M36]

D19		kiln	2s. *tꜣ* [U30]
D20		well full of water	2s. *ḥm* [N41]
D21		jar-stand	1s. *g* [W11]
D22		butcher's block	1s. *ḫ* [T28]
D23		stone jar	3s. *ẖnm* [W9]
D24		cup	det. cup, fluid [W10]
D25		pot	(1) 2s. *nw* (2) det. (?) in '(the goddess) Nekhbet' [W24]

§E Other tall signs

E1		throw-stick	det. foreign, hostile [T14]
E2		crook	3s. *ḥḳꜣ* [S38]
E3		club	2s. *ḥm* [U36]
E4		sceptre with forked end	3s. *wꜣs* [S40]
E5		E4 com. B15	abb. *wꜣst* '(city of) Thebes' [R19]
E6		standard with feather	det. or abb. *ỉmnt* 'west' and related words [R14]
E7		standard with spear	det. or abb. *ỉꜣbt* 'east' and related words [R15]
E8		standard	3s. *ỉꜣt* or *ꜣit* in the name *ḳꜣit* [R12]
E9		sceptre	3s. *sḫm* [S42]
E10		stone mace	2s. *ḥḏ* [T3]
E11		chisel	(1) 2s. *ꜣb* (2) 2s. *mr* [U23]
E12		stabbing sword	2s. *tp* [T8]
E13		arrow head	2s. *sn* [T22]
E14		pestle	2s. *ṯỉ* [U33]
E15		folded cloth	1s. *s* [S29]
E16		pennant	3s. *nṯr* or *ntr* [R8]
E17		three fox-skins	2s. *ms* [F31]
E18		crossed planks	3s. *ỉmy* or 2s. *ỉm* [Z11]
E19		sandal straps	3s. *ꜥnḫ* [S34]

E20		twisted wick	1s. *ḥ* [V28]
E21		water pot	2s. *ḥs* [W14]
E22		rack of water pots	3s. *ḫnt* [W17]
E22*		variant of E22	variant of E22 [W18]
E23		water pot with issue of contents	det. or abb. *ḳbḥ* 'artesian water' and related words [W15]
E24		E23 com. D21	abb. *ḳbḥw* 'Water-spring (region)' [W16]
E25		ointment jar	det. or abb. *mrḥt* 'ointment' [W1]
E25*		variant of E25	variant of E25 [W2]
E26		fire-drill	2s. *ḏꜣ* [U28]
E27		reed column	2s. *ḏd* [R11]
E28*		wooden column	2s. *ꜥꜣ* [O29]
E29		pillar	(1) 3s. *ỉwn* (2) abb. *ỉwnw* '(city of) Heliopolis' [W2]
E30		box-shrine	det. or abb. *sḥ* 'shrine' [O21]
E31		fringed cloth	det. or abb. *mnḫt* 'linen' [S27]
E32		steering oar	(1) 3s. *ḫrw* (2) 3s. *ḫpt* [P8]
E33		seat	2s. *ꜣs* [Q1]
E34		offering loaf	(1) 2s. *dỉ* or 1s. *d* (2) abb. *rdỉ* 'give' [X8]
E35		pot within a net	2s. *mỉ* [W19]
E36		writing equipment	det. or abb. *sẖ* 'write' [Y3]
E37*		papyrus plant	3s. *wꜣḏ* [M13]
E38*		heart and windpipe	3s. *nfr* [F35]

§F Other broad signs

F1		papyrus roll	det. writing, abstractions [Y1]
F2		basket with handle	1s. *k* [V31]
F3		basket	2s. *nb* [V30]
F4		stone vessel (?)	det. *ꜣbw* '(island of) Elephantine' [W8]

F5	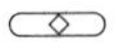	offering loaf	det. bread, offerings [X4]
F5*	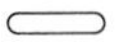	variant of F5	variant of F5
F6		loaf on mat	3s. *ḥtp* [R4]
F7		plan of house	(1) 2s. *pr* (2) det. building [O1]
F8	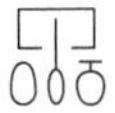	F7 com. E32 com. D16 com. D17	abb. *prt-ḫrw* 'voice-offering' [O3]
F9	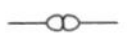	door bolt	1s. *s* [O34]
F10		pyramid-casing block	3s. *mꜣʿ* [Aa11]
F11		F12 com. F10	3s. *mꜣʿ* [U4]
F12		sickle	2s. *mꜣ* [U1]
F13		hoe	2s. *mr* [U7]
F13*		variant of F13	variant of F13 [U6]
F14		plough	3s. *šnʿ* [U13]
F15	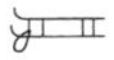	sledge	2s. *tm* [U15]
F16		adze on block	3s. *stp* [U21]
F17		harpoon	2s. *wʿ* [T21]
F18	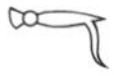	whip	2s. *mḥ* [V22]
F19		saw	det. or abb. *sḳ* or *sḳr* 'slice, slaughter' [Aa7]
F20		tusk	2s. *bḥ* [F18]
F21		tethering rope	1s. *ṯ* [V13]
F22		emblem of god Min	det. or abb. *mnw* '(the god) Min' [R23]
F24	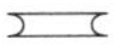	canal	2s. *mr* [N36]
F25		enclosure wall	abb. or det. wall [O36]
F26	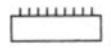	board game	2s. *mn* [Y5]
F27		gold collar	det. or abb. *nbw* 'gold' [S12]
F28	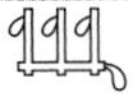	stylized toes	3s. *sꜣḥ* [D61]
F29	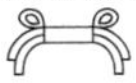	shoulder knot	2s. *sṯ* [S22]
F30		seal on necklace	abb. *ḫtmty* 'seal-bearer' [S19]

LIST OF WORDS IN HIEROGLYPHS

This is an index of all the words you have met in the book, including names of people and also names of gods, who are discussed in more detail on pages 141–44. The only words used in the book not listed here are names of kings, because these are discussed more fully in the relevant sections above and also listed on pages 136–40. However, kings' titles and epithets do appear in the index.

Following the standard practice in Egyptology, words have been listed in alphabetical order according to their transliteration (see **#9**). We do it this way because Egyptian words can often be written using entirely different hieroglyphs or combinations of hieroglyphs. As a result, listing words on the basis of how they appear in writing would be too confusing. Instead, each word is listed below with a typical hieroglyphic writing at the head of its entry, while common variations (other than the most straightforward variations) are also given. In this way, different writings of the same word are collected in a single entry. Occasionally, where the writing of a word presents particular problems, such as  for *nsw* 'king', cross-references are given to point you in the right direction.

Anyway, the standard alphabetical order for Egyptian is as follows:

ꜣ – ỉ – y – ꜥ – w – b – p – f – m – n – r – h – ḥ – ḫ – ẖ – s – š – ḳ – k – g – t – ṯ – d – ḏ

So to look up a word in this list (or any Egyptian dictionary), you need to know its transliteration. If you do not know some of the signs used to write the word, you can find them in a sign list, like the one on pages 144–53. For example, the first word below is . Suppose you came across this word in an inscription and recognized all the signs except . Then you would turn to the sign list (looking first in the list of Other Tall Signs), where you find  given as sign E11, which can read *ꜣb* or *mr*. The use of  suggests that *ꜣb* is correct here, so you can begin by looking in the index for a word with the letters *ꜣbw*. Sure enough, you will find that  *ꜣbw* is the name of the place we call Elephantine.

One technical point – for you not to worry about. Egyptian dictionaries usually ignore the feminine ending *-t* when listing words. However, the reasons for doing so do not affect us here, and this index does not follow that practice. On the other hand, you will notice that some pairs of masculine-feminine words have been listed together in the same entry, such as  *sꜣ* 'son' along with  *sꜣt* 'daughter'.

ꜣ	or *ꜣbw*	Elephantine (place)
	ꜣbḏw	Abydos (place)
	or *ꜣpd*	fowl
	ꜣsỉr	Osiris (god)
	ꜣst	Isis (goddess)
ỉ	or *ỉꜣbt*	east
	ỉy	Iy (name)
	ỉy	Iy (name)
	or *ỉwnw*	Heliopolis
	ỉby	Iby (name)
	ỉm	on; *ꜥnḫt nṯr ỉm* which a god lives on
	ỉmꜣḫy	as *ỉmꜣḫw* (see page 51)
	ỉmꜣḫw	revered one (see page 47)
	ỉmy	who is in; *ỉmy wt* who is in the *ut* (see page 142)
	or *ỉmn*	Amun (god)
	ỉmny	Ameny (name)
	ỉmnmḥꜣt	Amenemhat (name)
	ỉmntw	westerners, people of the west (i.e. the dead); (see **#20**)
	or *ỉn*	it is (specifies somebody who performs an action, see **#21**)
	or *ỉnpw*	Anubis (god)
	ỉntf	Intef (name)
	ỉr	do, make; *ỉr.n* made by (i.e. child of + parent's name) *ỉr.f dỉ ꜥnḫ* so he may carry out the given life (see **#26**)
	ỉsw	Yesu (name)
	or *ỉt*	father (see page 19)
	ỉdn	Iden (name)
y	*ywỉꜣ*	Yuia (name)
ꜥ	or ꜥꜣ	great; *nṯr ꜥꜣ* great god, *pr ꜥꜣ* great estate = palace (see page 82)
		see *ḏdt*
	or *ꜥnḫ*	life, live; *ꜥnḫ.tỉ* living, *ꜥnḫt nṯr ỉm* which a god lives on
	ꜥnḫw	Ankhu (name)
w	*wꜣs*	authority
	or *wꜣst*	Thebes (place)
	or *wꜣḏyt*	Wadjyt (goddess)
	or *wꜥ*	one, leader (?)
	or *wꜥb*	pure
	wꜥb	priest
	or *wḥmw*	messenger
	or *wsr*	power, powerful; Usret (goddess, see page 89)
	wḏꜣ-ꜣw	Wedjaaw (name)
	wt	*ut* (fetish used in shrines of Anubis); *ỉmy wt* who is in the *ut*
b	*bꜣ*	soul (see page 135)
	bỉk nbw	falcon of gold (see page 125)
	bỉty	king; *nsw-bỉty* dual king (see page 87)
p	*pw*	he/she is (see **#28**)
	pr	estate; *m-r pr* overseer of an estate (title), *pr ꜥꜣ* great estate = palace (see page 82)

	prt-ḫrw	voice offering; *dỉ.f prt-ḫrw* so that he may give a voice-offering (see page 54)
	pt	sky
	or *ptḥ*	Ptah (god); *ptḥskr* Ptah-Sokar (god)
f	*f*	he, his (attaches to the word it describes, see page **#15**)
m	or *m-r*	overseer; *m-r ḥm-nṯr* overseer of priests, *m-r pr* overseer of an estate, etc.
	or *mꜣꜥ*	true; *mꜣꜥ ḫrw* true of voice
	or or or or *mꜣꜥt*	divine order (see page 141)
	or *mỉ*	like; *mỉ rꜥ* like Ra
	or *mwt*	mother
	or *mnw*	Min (god)
	or *mnḫt*	linen
	mnṯw	Montju (god)
		see *nswmnṯw*
		see *m-r*
	or *mr*	love; or or *mry* beloved, *mrr.f* whom he loves (see pages 133–34)
	mrms	Mermose (name)
	mrrỉ	Mereri (name)
	mrrt	Mereret (name)
	or *mrḥt*	ointment
	mḥty	northern
	ms	give birth; *ms.n* born of (+ mother's name)
n	*n*	to, for
	n	of; *nt* of (see **#18**)
	nwt	Nut (goddess)
	or *nb*	lord (in titles); *nbt* lady, *nbty* twin ladies (see page 125), *nb-tꜣwy* lord of the twin lands, *nb-tꜣ ḏsr* lord of the sacred land, *nb-ḫꜥw* lord of appearances
	nb	all, every; *ḫt nbt* every thing
	nbw	gold
	nbtw	Nebtu (name)
	or *nfr*	perfect; *nṯr nfr* perfect god (see page 101)
	nfrt	Nefret (name)
	nhrynꜣ	Naharin (place)
	nht	sycamore
	or *nḫt*	strong
	nḫt	Nakht (name)
	or *nḫbt*	Nekhbet (goddess)
	nsw	king; *nsw-bỉty* dual king (see page 87), *ḥmt nsw* king's wife, *sꜣ nsw* king's son, *ḥtp dỉ nsw* offering which the king gives (see **#10**)
	nswmnṯw	Nesumontju (name)
	nṯr	god; *nṯr ꜥꜣ* great god (see **#20**), *nṯr nfr* perfect god (see page 101)
r	*r*	to, towards, at
	r	mouth
	or or *rꜥ*	sun, sun-god (= Ra), daytime; *mỉ rꜥ* like Ra
	rn	name

	rsy	southern
	rdỉ	give; *rdỉt* giving (see page 104), *dỉ ꜥnḫ* given life (see **#25**), *dỉ.f prt-ḫrw* so that he may give a voice-offering (see page 54)
h	*hp*	law
ḥ	*ḥꜣty-ꜥ*	governor
	ḥw	strike
	ḥtḥr	Hathor (goddess)
	ḥm	servant; king's servant (see page 115)
	ḥm-nṯr	priest
	ḥmt	wife; *ḥmt nsw* king's wife
	ḥnḳt	beer
	ḥr	above
	ḥr	keeper, chief; *ḥr sštꜣ* keeper of secrets (title)
	ḥrw	Horus (god)
	ḥs	praise; , *ḥss.f* whom he praises (see pages 133–34)
	ḥḳꜣ	ruler
	ḥtp	offer, offering; *ḥtp dỉ nsw* offering which the king gives (see **#10**), *dbḥt ḥtp* asked-for offerings
	ḥdrt	Hedjret (name)
ḫ	*ḫꜣ*	thousand
	ḫꜥ	appear; *ḫꜥw* appearances, *nb-ḫꜥw* lord of appearances
	ḫpr	form, being
	ḫpš	strength
	ḫnt	in front, ahead; *ḫnt ỉmntw* in front of the westerners, *ḫnt sḥ nṯr* in front at the god's booth
	ḫr	before
	ḫrw	voice; *prt ḫrw* voice offering, *mꜣꜥ ḫrw* true of voice
	ḫt	thing; *ḫt nbt* every thing
	ḫtmty	seal-bearer; *ḫtmty nṯr* god's seal-bearer (title)
ẖ	*ẖnmw*	Khnum (god)
	ẖnmwḥtp	Khnumhotep (name)
	ẖr	under, beneath
	ẖrt	course, duration
	ẖt	belly
s	*s*	she, her (attaches to the word it describes, see **#15**)
	s	man
	sꜣ	son; *sꜣt* daughter *sꜣ nsw* king's son *sꜣ rꜥ* son of Ra (see page 90)
	sꜣw	guardian
	sꜣtsbk	Satsobk (name)
	sꜥnḫ	keep alive
		see *nsw*
	sbk	Sobk (god)
	sp	occasion, event
	smn	establish
	smr	companion (title)
	sn	brother; *snt* sister
	snỉ	Seni (name)
	sntr	incense

	sḥ	booth; *sḥ nṯr* god's booth (for a statue)
	sḥḏ	controller; *sḥḏ ḥm nṯr* controller of priests
	sẖ	writing
	sšꜣt	Seshat (goddess)
	sštꜣ	secrets; *ḥry sštꜣ* keeper of secrets (title)
	sḳ	slice, slaughter
	skr	Sokar (god); *ptḥ-skr* Ptah-Sokar (god)
	sgrḥ	pacify, calm
	stp	choose; *stp.n* chosen by (see page 93)
	stt	Satet (goddess)
	sṯtw	Asiatics (people of the East)
š	*š*	lake
	šw	Shu (god)
	šmꜥ	south, Upper Egypt
	šnꜥ	storehouse
	šnwy	Shenwy (name)
	šs	alabaster
ḳ	*ḳꜣi̓t*	Qait (name)
	ḳbḥw	(artesian) water
	ḳbḥw	Water-spring (place, region south of Aswan)
k	*kꜣ*	ox
	kꜣ	soul
	kꜣw	food, sustenance
	kꜣry	Karoy (place)
	kšy	Kush, Cush (place)
g	*gb*	Geb (god)
t	*t*	bread
	tꜣ	land; *nb-tꜣwy* lord of the twin lands, *tꜣ ḏsr* sacred land (see page 111)
	tꜣš	boundary
	ty	Ty (name)
	tyy	Tiye (name)
	tp	on; *tp ḏw.f* upon his hill (see page 46)
	tpy	first
	tfnwt	Tefnut (goddess)
	tmw	Atum, Creator (see page 141)
ṯ	*ṯwi̓ꜣ*	Tjuia (name)
	ṯntt	temple-cattle
d		see *rdi̓*
	dwꜣmwtf	Duamutef (god)
	dwꜣt	afterlife (lit. state of adoration)
	dbḥ	request, ask for; *dbḥt ḥtp* asked-for offerings (see page 65)
	dn	crush
	ddw	Dedu (name)
	ddt	Dedet (name)
ḏ	*ḏw*	hill; *tp ḏw.f* upon his hill (see page 46)
	ḏḥwty	Thoth (god)
	ḏsr	sacred; *tꜣ ḏsr* sacred land
	ḏt	cobra (unless this is simply a writing of the goddess *wꜣḏyt*, see above)
	ḏd	stability
	ḏdw	Djedu (place)

SOURCES OF ILLUSTRATIONS

British Museum, London **112**, **119**; Culture and Sport Glasgow (Museums) **34**, **49**; Egyptian Museum, Cairo **114**, **118**; Fitzwilliam Museum, Cambridge **13**; Claire Gilmour **15**, **29**, **35**, **49**, **58**, **60**, **70**, **74**, **80**, **81**, **92**, **95**, **100**, **102**, **103**, **116**, **120**; From Selim Hassan, *The Great Sphinx and its Secrets. Historical Studies in the Light of Recent Excavations*. Excavations at Giza 8. (Cairo, Government Press, 1953), plate XLVIII 99; Louvre, Paris **84**; Dr William Manley **54**, **83**, **84**, **86**, **89**, **94**, **97**, **123**, **124**, **131**, **132**, **133**; Metropolitan Museum of Art, New York. Rogers Fund, 1916 (16.10.327). Photo 2011 Metropolitan Museum of Art/Art Resource/Scala, Florence **66**; Metropolitan Museum of Art, New York. Purchase, Joseph Pulitzer Bequest, 1960 (60.144). Purchase, Lila Acheson Wallace Gift, 1975 (1975.149). Photo 2011 Metropolitan Museum of Art/Art Resource/Scala, Florence **85**; National Museums Scotland **10**, **44**, **45**, **52**, **64**, **78**; Petrie Museum of Egyptian Archaeology, University College London **2–3**, **5–9**, **68**; Roger Wood **107**.

The hieroglyphic fonts used to print this work are available from Linguist's Software, Inc. PO Box 580, Edmonds, WA 98020-0580, USA. Telephone (425) 775-1130 www.linguistsoftware.com

INDEX

Italic numerals refer to the page numbers of illustrations and their captions.